John Shebbeare

An Answer to the Printed Speech of Edmund Burke

spoken in the House of commons, April 19, 1774: in which his knowledge in polity,

legislature, humankind, history, commerce and finance, is candidly examined

John Shebbeare

An Answer to the Printed Speech of Edmund Burke
spoken in the House of commons, April 19, 1774: in which his knowledge in polity, legislature, humankind, history, commerce and finance, is candidly examined

ISBN/EAN: 9783337878719

Printed in Europe, USA, Canada, Australia, Japan

Cover: Foto ©Andreas Hilbeck / pixelio.de

More available books at **www.hansebooks.com**

A

A N S W E R

TO THE

PRINTED SPEECH

OF

EDMUND BURKE, Efq;

SPOKEN IN THE

Houfe of Commons, *April* 19, 1774.

IN WHICH

His Knowledge in Polity, Legiflature, Humankind, Hiftory, Commerce and Finance, is candidly examined; his Arguments are fairly refuted; the Conduct of Adminiftration is fully defended; and his Oratoric Talents are clearly expofed to view.

ADDRESSED TO THE PEOPLE.

Eft etiam in quibufdam turba inanium verborum, qui dum communem loquendi morem reformidant, ducti fpecie nitoris, circumeunt omnia copiofa loquacitate quæ dicere volunt. QUINTILIAN, l. 8. ch. 2.

. . . . nec lex eft æquior ulla
Quam necis artifices arte perire fua. OVID.

For rhetoric he cou'd not ope
His mouth, but out there flew a trope,
This he as volubly wou'd vent
As if his ftock would ne'er be fpent;
And truely to fupport that charge,
He had fupplies as vaft and large;
For he cou'd coin, or counterfeit
New words with little or no wit.

HUDIBRAS.

LONDON:

Printed for T. EVANS, near *York-Buildings*, in the *Strand*; and J. BEW, No. 28, in *Pater-nofter Row*. M.DCC.LXXV.

[Price Three Shillings and Sixpence.]

PREFACE.

HAD the speech of Mr. Burke been shorter, or less open to refutation, this answer would have been shorter also. But when every page is replete with such things as were too singular to be unobserved; when a selecting of particular passages would have borne the face of a partial and disingenuous enquiry, it was thought more eligible to be just than concise, and to refute the whole; since the whole was refutable. Had either his knowledge of the subjects, on which he spoke, the arguments which he adduced, or the powers of oratory, which he is thought to possess, been unexamined, the part omitted would have been pronounced, by his hardy associates, to be unanswerable. On that account, the examination has been carried thro' the whole; and the length of it must be ascribed to Mr. Burke. Besides this, as it contains,

tains, not only an anfwer to this fpeech, but to all that has been offered by the patriots on that fubject, it may be of ufe to both fides of the queftion; and as it includes the hiftory alfo of all that important tranfaction, it may not unlikely be of fervice to remove the prejudices of the deluded; and to eftablifh the fentiments of the well-difpofed. Of this I am convinced. It will prove that his majefty and his miniftry are engaged in defending the dignity of the realm, and the rights of the people, and be *"a full refutation of the charges of that party with which Mr. Burke has all along acted."* The editor of this anfwer, hath not kept it back, from a *delicacy poffibly over fcrupulous:* but the publication hath been retarded, more than a month, by a fit of the gout, that was not *over fcrupuloufly delicate.*

A N

A N

A N S W E R

To the SPEECH of

Edmund Burke, Efq;

IT has been a long, an univerfal, and a juft complaint, that the fenate-houfe, in which your
Reprefentatives affemble, is not only too fmall to
contain the whole number of the members; but
that you, the community of this kingdom, are
thereby precluded from being prefent on thofe occafions that are the moft interefting to your welfare. Not the fmallnefs of your houfe alone, the
perverfenefs of your fervants alfo, augments the
impracticability of your being truly informed of
what is therein tranfacted. Nothing is authentically

B   given

given to the public. Even the admiffion of one man, who might commit their inimitable harangues to paper, is prohibited. In confequence of thefe circumftances, all the means, of obtaining a genuine information of what each fenator delivers, are abfolutely refcinded. Ignorance, prefumption, party-fpirit, envy and felf-intereft, either feparately or in conjunction, prepofterously exalt, or fcandaloufly depreciate the performances of your fpeakers, according to the difpofitions and views of thofe who report them : fo that their intrinfic merit is feldom to be known. On this account, it is juftly your ardent wifh that the patriots would publifh their fpeeches under their own infpection; and prevent the barbarifm of the London Evening Poft, and other papers, from mutilating that precious offspring which hath coft them fo much care and ftudy to bring into the world; and which you are not permitted to fee but in detached parts and diffevered limbs.

Mr. Burke, touched with paternal tendernefs for your welfare, and confcious that it is the duty of every upright member to comply with your defires, unactuated by vanity or malevolence, hath gracioufly led the way to the demolition of that unconftitutional practice : and hath given you in print that celebrated Oration which he delivered on the 19th of laft April, with fo much applaufe, from his own patriotic party. It appears from the Preface to this oration, " that it was much the fubject of " converfation, and that the defire of having it print- " ed *laft fummer* was very general ;" and therefore you were prefented with it *this winter*. You are informed alfo, "that the means of gratifying the " public curiofity were obligingly furnifhed from the " notes of fome gentlemen, members of the laft

par-

" parliament ; that it has been many months ready
" for the prefs; but that a delicacy, poffibly over-
" fcrupulous, has delayed the publication to this
" time."

It is extremely natural for men of *a delicacy fo*
over fcrupulous, and fo free from vanity, as Mr.
Burke will appear to be in the examination of this
Speech, to apologize for fuch things; as others of
more confident difpofitions give to the world,
without the leaft diffidence or hefitation.

Notwithftanding what has been juft faid, refpecting the *means* furnifhed from the notes of
other gentlemen ; this Speech is not to be confidered to be in print, as it fell from the lips of the
Orator in the houfe of commons. But as having
received the utmoft finifhing and perfection which
he can give to his rhetorical performances. It is
manifeftly on a fubject not unpremeditated. It is
the full refult of *nine years* ftudy. It may therefore be juftly deemed to include a complete exhibition of thofe oratoric excellences which he fo
eminently poffeffes : and from hence his merits may be accurately known, and truly afcer-
tained. Rafh as the undertaking may be deemed.
Unterrified by the fate which fell on Æfchines,
when he arraigned Demofthenes, the moft celebrated of the Grecian orators, " it is a fpeech fo
" chequered and fpeckled ; a piece of joinery fo
" crofsly indented and whimfically dove-tailed ; a
" cabinet fo varioufly inlaid ; fuch a piece of diver-
" fified Mofaic ; fuch a teffelated pavement without
" cement :"* *I'll crofs it though it blaft me.*

B 2

This

---

* It is an admonition of Longinus, that whoever would
write on any fubject fhould previoufly confider, in what manner the moft eminent authors have delivered themfelves on

fimilar

This Speech was delivered in anſwer to what had been ſpoken by Mr. Cornwall, on *a motion to take into conſideration the duty of Three-pence per pound weight upon Tea, payable in all his majeſty's American dominions.* On this queſtion, and in this harangue, the Orator has taken occaſion to introduce a pompous panegyric on his Maſter and himſelf; and to reprehend, with his natural *over-ſcrupulouſneſs of delicacy,* the conduct of all other miniſters. " He tells you, it contains a full refutation of " the charges againſt that party with which Mr. " Burke has all along acted ; the ſubject is inte- " reſting ; the matters of information various and " important." It therefore claims your ſtricteſt attention.

He begins, " I agree with the honourable gen- " tleman, who ſpoke laſt, that this ſubject is not
" new

ſimilar occaſions, and emulate their manner of thinking and expreſſion. I have obſerved that rule. I have ſelected Mr. Burke, and more than imitated him, in the paſſage to which this note refers. There are, indeed, both a ſimilarity and diſſimilarity, between Longinus and Mr. Burke, extremely remarkable. Both of them have written on the ſublime. The Grecian practiſed the preceding rule, *and was himſelf the great ſublime he drew.* The Hybernian practiſes that rule alſo. So far they reſemble. But then he follows the examples of writers who are of another ſtamp. In forming this Oration the ΠΕΡΙ ΒΑΘΟΥΣ of Martinus Scriblerus was continually before his eyes, as it ſhall be ſhewn in a number of notes in this anſwer. Longinus was ſecretary to Zenobia, queen of the Palmyrians. Mr. Burke to a Firſt Lord of the Treaſury. Longinus prevailed on his miſtreſs not to yield to the demands of the emperor Aurelian : but to defend her dominions to the laſt extremity. Mr. Burke perſuaded his maſter to flee from before the face of rebels, and to grant their lawleſs demands without contention. Longinus was infamouſly put to death for this virtuous and heroic conduct. Mr. Burke is ſtill alive, and juſtifying that tranſaction, which ſo ſignally diſgraced his maſter and injured this country. Such is their diſſimilitude.

" new to this houfe, very difagreeable to this houfe,
" very unfortunately to this nation, and to the peace
" and profperity of this whole empire; no topic has
" been more familiar to us, for *nine long years*;
" feffion after feffion, we have been lafhed round and
" round this miferable circle of occafional arguments
" and temporary expedients. I am fure our heads
" muft turn and our ftomachs naufeate with them.
" We have had them in every fhape; we have look-
" ed at them in every point of view; invention is
" exhaufted; reafon is fatigued; experience has giv-
" en judgement; but obftinacy is not yet con-
" quered."

From this paffage, it is evident that his fpeech
includes, not only the fruits of *nine years voluntary
labour*, but all that could be *whipped* out of him
by a *nine years lafhing* alfo. Within fix lines he
plunges into metaphor; conjoins thofe *arguments*
and *expedients* which never can be brought to touch;
and bends the *inflexible progreffion* of *time* and *occafion* into a circle,* round which the commons,
like affes working in a mill, are miferably lafhed
for nine long years. No wonder then their heads
grow giddy, and their ftomachs naufeate thofe
arguments and expedients. And altho' he tells you
they have been *conftantly* lafhed in this *one* miferable
circle, "they have neverthelefs had them in *every*
"*fhape*," fquare, triangle, ifofceles, polygon, and

B 3   fcalenum;

* And I will venture to lay it down as the firft maxim and
corner ftone of this our art, that whoever would excel therein, muft ftudiouhly avoid, deteft, and turn his head from all
the ideas, ways, and workings of that peftilent foe to wit,
and *deftroyer of five figures*, which is known by the name of *common fenfe*: his bufinefs muft be to contract the true *gout de
travers*, and to acquire a moft happy, uncommon, unaccountable way of thinking.
Bathos. C. 5th. of the true genius for the profound.

ſcalenum. And although invention be exhauſt-
ed ; reaſon fatigued ; experience hath given judgment; 'and the ſubject hath turned the heads
and ſtomachs of the members ; all which are reaſons for *his* obſervation of inſuperable ſilence ;
he nevertheleſs begins a *new laſhing* by a ſpeech of
two hours duration, and demonſtrates that *his* ob-
ſtinacy is not yet conquered. Such is the wonderful conſiſtency with which this incomparable
ſpeaker begins and ends' his matchleſs exordium.

However, he tells you, "the honourable gentle-
" man has made one endeavour more to diverſify
" the form of this diſguſting *argument*." What argument? he has mentioned none. But he ex-
plains himſelf, " he has thrown out a ſpeech com-
" poſed almoſt entirely of challenges. Challenges
" are ſerious things : and as he is a man of prudence
" as well as reſolution, he dares to ſay Mr. Cornwal
" has very well weighed thoſe challenges before he
" delivered them." This and " the ſubmiſſion of
" his *poor* opinions to the houſe," are undoubtedly
intended to be ironically received. For had his
opinion of Mr. Cornwall been ſo *great*, and of
himſelf ſo *poor*, would it not have been an unpar-
donable temerity to have undertaken to anſwer
thoſe challenges which the former had thrown
out ? eſpecially when it will be ſhewn how prudent it had been, had he never accepted them.

Mr. Cornwall " has ſtated to the houſe," as the
orator informs you, "two grounds of deliberati-
" on, one narrow and ſimple, and merely confined
" to the queſtion on the paper; the other more large
" and more complicated, comprehending the whole
" ſeries of the parliamentary proceedings, with re-
" gard to America, their cauſes, and their cohſe-
" quences." It is acknowledged by the ancients,

who

who have written beſt on the ſubjeᴄt of oratory, that figures juſtly formed and happily introduced give an elevation to a ſpeech that cannot be at‑ tained by any other rhetorical powers. This idea hath not been concealed from this ſpeaker. And as he conſtantly adheres to *Mortyn*, as his arche‑ type of excellence, what office can be more agreeable to him than that of evincing how perfeᴄtly he is maſter of his favourite author. Hence it is he chooſes to *ſtate* the *grounds*. To *ſtate* a *queſtion*, a *propoſition*, or a *caſe* ; and *to lay out grounds* would be a deviation into common ſenſe and good Engliſh, which is contrary to the doc‑ trine of the celebrated Scriblerus, who ſays he can‑ not too earneſtly recommend his authors the ſtudy of the *abuſe of ſpeech*.* A ground may be alſo *narrow*, it may be *rough* or *ſmooth*, *ſteep* or *plain*, but a *ſim‑ ple* ground is *new*. And does it not ſeem difficult to conceive how the larger ground which *com‑ prehends* the whole *ſeries* of parliamentary procee‑d‑ ings, their cauſes, and conſequences, the moſt *regular* and *uniform* of all ſucceſſions, can be a *com‑. plicated ground?* and ſince the larger ground does comprehend this *whole* ſeries with regard to America, what occaſion could there be to ſtate *two* grounds, a leſs and a bigger, when the whole is included in the laſt ? I ſuſpeᴄt this happy thought was taken from the perſon who, having a large and a little cat, cut two holes in his door of different ſizes, becauſe he did not con‑ ceive that the *little cat* could go through the *large* hole.† " With regard to the latter ground, Mr.

B 4   " Cornwal

* Bathos. Ch. 10. of tropes and figures, in the catachreſis, *mow the beard, ſhave the graſs, pin the plank, nail my ſleeve.*

† Bathos, c. 9. of imitation. Imitation is of two ſerts ; 1ſt, when force to our own purpoſes the thoughts of others. The 2d conſiſts in copying imperfeᴄtions and blemiſhes.

" Cornwal, he fays, *ftates* it as ufelefs, and thinks it
" may be even dangerous to enter into fo extenfive
" a field of enquiry. Yet to his furprize he had hardly
" laid down this reftrictive propofition, to which his
" authority would have given fo much weight, when
" directly and with the fame authority he condemns
" it, and declares it abfolutely neceffary to enter into
" the moft ample hiftorical detail. His zeal has
" thrown him out of his ufual accuracy. He has re-
" probated in one part of his fpeech, the rule he had
" laid down for debate in the other, and after nar-
" rowing the ground for all thofe who are to fpeak
" after him, he takes an excurfion himfelf, as un-
" bounded as the fubject and the extent of his great
" abilities."

There is nothing which more effentially expofes
a fpeaker to ridicule than a pleafantry on others,
founded on a want of comprehenfion in himfelf.
Such is the prefent cafe. He hath defcribed Mr.
Cornwal as contradicting himfelf in ftating an enquiry into the larger ground, as dangerous: and
then, in declaring it abfolutely neceffary to enter
into the moft ample hiftorical detail ; and in re-
probating the rule in one part, which he had laid
down in another. On what is this affertion founded? Mr. Cornwal afferts, " that retrofpect is not
" wife; and the proper, the only proper fubject of
" enquiry is, *not how they got into this difficulty, but*
" *how they are to get out of it.*"

Such are the words, on which he has founded
his charge of Mr. Cornwal's want of accuracy.
Do *thefe* words, which limit the fubject to the *future*
means of extrication *only*, declare the neceffity of
returning to an *hiftorical* detail of what *was paft*?
do thefe enlarge the ground " to the comprehenſion

fion of the whole feries of parliamentary proceedings. with regard to America, their caufes and confequences," which abfolutely interdict all retrofpect, and urge the attention of the houfe to *fubfequent* confiderations only? "*has not his zeal thrown him more than a little into his ufual inaccuracy?*" Not content with this exhibition of his mifconception, he prefumes to give an explanatory fenfe to thofe words of Mr. Cornwal, which no comment can render more plain. And then, by the natural obliquity of his underftanding, he fucceeds as happily in this atempt as in the preceding. " In other words, fays he, we are, according to " Mr. Cornwal, to confult our invention, and to re- " ject our experience." Thefe, indeed, are not only *other words,* but they convey *other ideas* than an intellect merely human can derive from thofe of Mr. Cornwal. They neither direct you to *confult invention,* nor to *reject experience.* On the contrary, in faying, the only proper enquiry is, *how to get out of that difficulty,* do they exclude experience, reafon, common fenfe; and tell you to confult *invention* only? I will undertake, with the chemift in the flying ifland, to extract fun-beams out of cucumbers, and fucceed in it too, whenever Mr. Burke's fignification fhall be extracted from Mr. Cornwal's words. In his explanation, however, this reprehenfive orator hath manifeftly excluded not only reafon, common fenfe, and experience, but fhown the impotence of his invention alfo.

In proportion as he errs in judgment, he improves in peremptorinefs. " This mode of deli- " beration, which Mr. Cornwal recommends, he af- " ferts, is diametrically oppofite to every rule of " reafon, and every principle of good fenfe eftablifh- " ed

"ed among mankind. For that sense, and that rea-
" son, *he* hath *always* understood, absolutely to pre-
" scribe, whenever we are involved in difficulties,
" from the measures we have pursued, that we
" should take a strict review of those measures, in
" order to correct our errors, if they should be cor-
" rigible."

It is requisite that I once more bring before
you the words of Mr. Cornwal. " *The proper,
the only proper enquiry is, not how we got into this
difficulty, but how we are to get out of it.*" Do
these words, which state the object of the enquiry,
to be, *how to get out of the difficulty,* recommend
or convey the least idea of the MODE of deliberation? Hence it is evident, he mistakes the *fashion*
for the substance of which it is *formed.* Is it not
necessary that a man should understand the words
he utters before he presume to be an orator? but
to experience I appeal, the judge which he asserts
Mr. Cornwal hath rejected, whether it " be so
diametrically opposite to every rule of *reason* and
every principle of *good sense* established among
mankind."

If any man, by carelessly sleeping, and leaving his candle unextinguished, should set his bed
on fire, and waking, find himself surrounded with
the flame, do *reason* and *good sense* absolutely
prescribe, that he should take a strict review of
the measures by which he was involved in that
difficulty, before he attempts to get out of it? If the
house should take fire, and the engines be ready
to extinguish it, is it opposite to every rule of *reason,* and every principle of *good sense,* to suffer
the engines to play before the proprietor hath
taken a strict review of the measures which involved him in that difficulty? if a mariner, by an
er-

erroneous reckoning, find himself, at day-break, on a lee-shore, and that his vessel hath sprung a leak, do *reason* and *good sense* absolutely prescribe that, before he attempts to get off that shore, and to stop the leak, he should take a strict review of the measures that brought him into those difficulties? In these cases, and innumerable others, would not such a mode of deliberation be opposite to every *rule of reason*, and every *principle of good sense*, established among mankind?

But although the experience of mankind, and the very exposure of this opinion, do manifest its absurdity; I am nevertheless convinced, that this Orator has constantly understood, that it is right. Because, through his whole speech, he undeviatingly sees all objects in an inverted order. And, from this instance, is it not a fair inference, that his *reason* and *good sense* are in contrast with those of all other men : and that he is the only person who possesses both in perfection? but he is too delicate to deliver that opinion. You shall see it, however, in his practice. For were his opinion to be adopted, every fire must be a general conflagration of that place in which it happens. Plagues must spread through kingdoms, because every *rule* of *reason*, every *principle* of *good sense* interdicts the means of stopping their progress, until the measures be strictly reviewed, by which they were brought into them. And thus, according to his wisdom, the world would speedily be involved in difficulties irremediable. These are indisputably invincible reasons for coinciding with his opinion, and for rejecting that of Mr. Cornwal. They prove also, how admirably his intellect is adapted to *guide* a minister who is to *guide* the
state ;

ſtate; or to execute that object of his ambition, the
ſole guidance of it, by his own faculties. For
who can be more adequately ſelected for ſo important a duty than a man who, on *principle*, would
permit the enemy to land without oppoſition, until he had taken a ſtrict review of thoſe meaſures by
which the nation was involved in that difficulty?

Such being the reſult of his underſtanding, in
the preceding inſtance, he adds, " he will freely
" follow Mr. Cornwal in his hiſtorical diſcuſſion,
" without the leaſt management for men or mea-
" ſures, farther than they ſhall ſeem to him to de-
" ſerve it." I will follow *his* example, reſpecting
himſelf, and all others. I will obſerve him as a
ſupervíſor does an exciſeman; examine his accounts; expoſe his errors to your inſpection, and
" omit nothing which can give you ſatisfaction."
Only that I will not *tread* " the *narrow ground*,"
but the *narrow path*; becauſe I will not follow him
in the *exquiſiteneſs* of his *tropes*.

Mr. Cornwal, as the Orator affirms, " deſires
" to know, whether, if the houſe were to repeal this
" tax, agreably to the propoſition of the motion,
" the Americans would not take poſt on this condi-
" tion, in order to make a new attack on the next
" body of taxes; and whether they would not call
" for a repeal of the duty on wines, as loudly as
" they do now for the duty on Teas?" And thus,
according to the ideas of this ſpeaker, a queſtion
on what may be the events of *futurity*, is an *hiſtorical* diſcuſſion of what is *paſt*; which, unleſs a man
may write the *hiſtory* of things that *never* have happened, as well as ſpeak on ſubjects which he never
underſtood ſeems to be incomprehenſible. Did Mr.
Cornwal expreſs himſelf in a manner ſo incongruous?
did he convert a *conceſſion* into a plain of *terra firma*,
and

and poft the Americans thereon, in line of battle, to attack the next *body of taxes*, which, by profopo-pœia, are converted into an *army*, to be affailed by thofe Americans? It is fo truly *Burkean* in the conception and the ftile, that I cannot, in confcience, pilfer him of the merit of that beautiful act of imagination, although his modefty afcribes it to Mr. Cornwal. For fuch is the characteriftic excellence of this fpeaker, that his *words fly* from his *lips* like race-horfes; whilft his *ideas* ftand *ftock-ftill* in his *brain*, like fpectators at the ftarting-poft.

Mr. Cornwal afks a plain queftion; "what " would be the event of repealing the Tea duty ?" Mr. Burke, in anfwer, replies, " he can give no " fecurity on that fubject." He was afked his opinion on what might happen in America? he anfwers, as if he were required to give an obligation to pay a debt in England. " He can give no *fe-* " *curity*." He is afked one queftion, and returns an anfwer which belongs to another. However, "he " will do all he can, and all that can be fairly de- " manded. To the *experience* which Mr. Cornwal " reprobates, in one inftance, and reverts to in the " next, to that *experience*, without the leaft waver- " ing or hefitation, on his part, he fteadily appeals." You have already feen his fuccefs in appealing to experience, in the antecedent inftance. You will foon perceive a like effect in this alfo; and find that it has given judgment againft him. For it now appears, that the *experience*, which Mr. Cornwal *re-jected* for *invention*, was neverthelefs *not rejected*, but *reprobated*, for one inftant, and *reverted* to in the next. But it is the fingular fate of this fpeaker, to be uniformly in one feries of felf-contradiction. However, this is his anfwer. "When parliament repealed " the Stamp-act, in the year, 1766, he affirms, firft; " that

" that the Americans did *not*, in confequence of this
" meafure, call upon them to give up the former
" parliamentary revenue, which fublifted in that
" country." That they did not, at that time, call
upon parliament, in order to obtain a furrender of
the former revenues, is true ; and the reafons
which withheld them fhall be fhewn, when I come
to lay the Rockingham adminiftration before you.
It is to be remarked alfo, that this appeal is not
to *experience*, but to the Orator *himfelf*;. and how
well he is inftructed by *experience* has been already
evinced.

He continues his appeal to the fame experience,
and " affirms alfo, that when departing from the
" maxims of the repeal, the Commons revived the
" fcheme of taxation, and thereby filled the minds
" of the colonifts with frefh jealoufy, and all forts of
" apprehenfions, then it was they quarrelled with
" the old taxes as well as the new ; then it was, and
" not till then, that they queftioned all the parts of
" your legiflative power, and by the *battery* of fuch
" *queftions*, have fhaken the folid ftructure of this
" empire to its deepeft foundations."

That this ftrenuous affirmation of Mr. Burke
is not the refult of experience, I fhall prove from
that which experience dictated to an indifputable
judge, the governor of the province of Maffachufets. In his letter dated Feb. 28, 1776, he
fays " the *ftamp* act is become, in *itfelf*, a *mattter* of
" *indifference* : it is fwallowed up in the importance
" of the effects of what it has been the caufe, the
" taxing of the *Americans* by parliament has brought
" their very fubjection to the crown of *Great Britain*
" in queftion. To reconcile this, and to afcertain
" the nature of the fubjection of the colonies to the
" crown of *Great-Britain*, will be a work of time
and

" and difficulty, even though the ftamp-act fhould
" be removed to pave the way; the people
" have felt their ftrength, and flatter themfelves
" that it is much greater than it is, and will not
" fubmit readily to any thing they do not like."

Such was his opinion before the repeal of that
act; you fhall fee how it was confirmed by that
which followed it, in his letter of January the
28th, 1768; he tells you, " I underftand that it
" is a prevailing opinion, on your fide the ocean,
" that America, if left alone, will come to herfelf,
" and return to the fame fenfe of duty and obedi-
" ence to *Great-Britain*, which fhe poffeffed before
" the ftamp-act. But when the difpute has been
" carried fo far as to involve in it matters of the
" higheft importance to the *imperial fovereignty*;
" when it has produced queftions which the *fovereign*
" ftate cannot give up, and the *dependent* ftates infift
" upon as terms of reconciliation; when the *im-*
" *perial* ftate has fo far given way as to let the *de-*
" *pendent* ftates flatter themfelves, that their pre-
" tenfions are admiffible; whatever terms of recon-
" ciliation time, accident, or defign may produce,
" if they are deficient in fettling the true relation of
" *Great-Britain* to her *colonies*, and afcertaining the
" bounds of the *fovereignty* of one, and the *de-*
" *pendence* of the other, conciliation will be no more
" than fufpenfion of hoftilities. It was eafy to be
" forefeen that the diftinctions ufed in parliament,
" in favour of the Americans, would be adopted by
" them, and received as fundamental laws.

" Let us ftate the pofitions urged in parliament
" on the behalf of the Americans. It was faid in
" parliament, that 1ft, the parliament have no right
" to tax the Americans, becaufe the Americans have
" no reprefentatives in parliament. 2d, But they
" have

" have a right to impofe *port duties*, or *external*
" taxes, becaufe fuch duties are for the regulation
" of trade. 3d, The difference between an *external*
" and *internal* tax is, that the former is impofed for
" the regulation of trade, and the latter for raifing a
" revenue. From thefe premifes, the Americans
" have drawn the following conclufions, 1. *port
" duties* impofed for raifing a revenue are *internal*
" taxes. 2. *Port duties*, of which the produce is
" to be paid into the exchequer for the ufe of go-
" vernment, are impofed for raifing a revenue.
" 3. The produce of all the port duties, impofed
" on America is ordered to be paid into the ex-
" chequer for the ufe of government. 4. All the
" *port duties* impofed on America are *internal* taxes.
" The only difference between the *port duties*, de-
" clared to be for raifing a revenue, and thofe of
" which no fuch declaration is made, is, that in one,
" the intention is explicit: in the other, it is im-
" plied. They both come within the definition of
" internal taxes; and there are no taxes left for the
" diftinction to operate upon. This is not a ficti-
" tious argument but a real one, now urged and in-
" fifted upon as the terms of a good agreement be-
" tween *Great-Britain* and her colonies."

Such is the experience to which I appeal. Such
is the evidence which confronts this orator. An
evidence which from his fpeech confeffedly appears to have been feen by him; and acknowledged
to be authentic. An evidence that proves that
the Americans quarrelled with the *old* taxes
as well as the *new*, not only after but before the
ftamp-act was repealed: and that thefe quarrels
were not only produced by the debates in parliament before it was enacted; but that they were
encreafed by the repeal of that act *which flattered*
them

them that their pretensions were admissible. This evidence, to which he offers no disproof, he hardily contradicts ; and confidently affirms " that not till after the revival of the laſt taxation, that then it was, and not till then they queſtioned all the parts of your legiſlative power." Such is the iſſue of his appeal to experience ; it gives the lye direct to all he has affirmed. Whether you conclude therefore that vanity hath turned his head ; deſperation hath urged him to this affirmation ; or want of intellect hath rendered him incapable to comprehend the meaning of the preceding letters from that governor, who, was witneſs to theſe American actions, will you longer liſten to him who thus affirms what facts diſprove ; and be deluded by ſuch aſſertions as carry with them their own refutation ? but you have already ſeen and will ſee, in a multiplicity of inſtances, that it is the diſtinguiſhing characteriſtic of this ſpeaker, to *affirm* without *proof* ; *revile* without *cauſe* ; *defend* without *argument* ; and *conclude* without *reaſon*.

But amidſt the croud of his affirmations, he ſhall not charge me with inobſervance on the excellence of his *figures*. " It was by the *battery of ſuch queſtions* of your legiſlative power, the Americans have ſhaken the ſolid ſtructure of this empire to its deepeſt foundations." A battery of *charges*, a battery of *aſſertions*, a battery of *accuſations*, may be a ſupportable metaphor : but a *battery* of *queſtions* is abſolutely irreconcilable with every idea of attacks by artillery. And yet " the ſolid ſtructure of this empire was ſhaken from its foundations by a *battery* of American *queſtions*." Why will the pertinaciouſneſs of the miniſtry perſevere in ſupporting the dignity of this empire, when it is evident, from this orator, it is now fun-

C   damentally

damentally fhaken? and will it not be totally fubverted by a fecond difcharge of that tremendous
battery of *queftions*? On this occafion, and in conformity with truth, I muft candidly declare, that it
was a manifeft injuftice to this incomparable
fpeaker, to fay his *invention* was exhaufted. Is it
not undeniable, that *he* clearly ftands the inventor
of this new and formidable improvement in artillery?

He perfifts, refpecting the conduct of the Americans, after the repeal of the ftamp act; and
chriftening his *affirmations* by the appellation of
propofitions, he fays, " of thofe two propofitions, I
"fhall before I have done give fuch damning proof,
" that however the contrary may be whifpered in
" circles, or bawled in news papers, they never
" more will dare to raife their voices in this houfe."*
Here again you fee a frefh inftance of his inven-
tive faculties. He has imagined the *propofitions* to be
two perfons; the firft to *whifper* in *circles*, and the
fecond to *bawl* in *news papers*, and then affures you
"they never more will dare to *raife their voices* in your
houfe." And thus he makes them members of parliament alfo: or the whole paffage is one piece of un-
grammaitcal ftuff, commonly called nonfenfe. As
to his fecond propofition, " that the minds of the
colonifts were not filled with jealoufy and apprehenfions, that they quarrelled not with the old
taxes, nor queftioned all the parts of the legiflative power, until the fcheme of the new taxation
was arrived;" I have already given him fuch proof
as hath already damned his affirmation. It fhall be
confirmed in the fubfequent parts of this anfwer,
and

* Bathos, chap. 10. in metonimy, the inverfion of caufes
for effects.

and the firft fhall inevitably follow the fame road, and both be damned together.

" I fpeak, fays he, with great confidence." His confidence is great indeed. Yet had not his *overfcrupulous delicacy* withheld him, his fpeaking might have juftly borne a more expreffive epithet. He adds alfo, " he has reafon for it." A truth indifputable, fince by the affiftance of *that* alone he can entertain the leaft hope to be freed from the embarraffments of his damning proofs.

Mark how vigoroufly he advances, fuftained by his powerful ally. " The minifters are with me, " they at leaft are convinced that the repeal of the " ftamp act, had not, and that no repeal can have " the confequences which Mr. Cornwall, who de- " fends their meafures is fo much alarmed at. To " their conduct I refer him for a conclufive anfwer " to his objection. He carries his proof irrefiftibly "into the very body of both miniftry and parliament, " not on any general reafoning, growing out of col- " lateral matter, but on the conduct of Mr. Corn- " wal's minifterial friends on the new revenue itfelf."

This indeed is fpeaking with great confidence. Proofs which have hitherto been carried into the *minds*, are by him carried irrefiftibly into the very *bodies* of the minifters and parliament. At firft I imagined this image had been taken from the prowefs of Sir John Falftaffe, who *bore his point* fo irrefiftibly into the bodies of feven buckram men, out of eleven of his own creation, whom he never touched : for there is a wonderful affinity to be feen between that fword of the knight, and the proofs of the orator. They enter nothing and are equally irrefiftible. In both inftances, all is buckram of their own invention. But on a fecond confiderati- on, it incontrovertibly appears, that this image of

car-

carrying his *proofs* irrefiftibly into the *bodies* of minifters and parliament men, is taken from the mode,
which he has reprefented to have been fo *irrefiftible*
in Mr. Charles Townfhend, and which will be
fhewn in this anfwer.

He proceeds to delineate the conduct of the miniftry, and on that conduct to carry his irrefiftible
proofs into their bodies. "The act of 1757,
" which grants this tea duty, fets forth in its pre-
" amble, that it was expedient to raife a revenue in
" America, for the fupport of the civil government
" there, *as well as for purpofes ftill more extenfive.*
" *To this fupport the act affigns fix branches of duties.*
" *About two years after this act paffed, the miniftry,*
" *I mean the prefent miniftry, thought it expedient to*
" *repeal five of the duties, and to leave (for reafons beft*
" *known to themfelves) only the fixth ftanding. Sup-*
" *pofe any perfon, at the time of that repeal, had thus*
" *addreffed lord North. Condemning, as you do, the*
" *repeal of the ftamp act, why do you venture to repeal*
" *the duties upon paper, glafs, and painter's colours ?*
" *let your pretence for the repeal be what it will, are*
" *you not thoroughly convinced, that your conceffions will*
" *produce, not fatisfaction, but infolence in the Ame-*
" *ricans; and that the giving up thefe taxes will neceffi-*
" *tate the giving up of all the reft.* This objection
" was as palpable then as it is now; and it was as
" good for preferving the five duties as for retaining
" the fixth. Upon the principles therefore of Mr.
" Cornwal, upon the principles of the minifter him-
" felf, the minifter has nothing to anfwer." Greatly
confident, as this affertion muft appear in him, I
am equally confident that the minifter had not only
an anfwer, but a perfect refutation of what that
fpeaker fo peremptorily afferts. The anfwer is fo
obvious, that even I fhall prefume to give it. An

an-

answer which would be altogether needless, had
this gentleman been acquainted with those *reasons*
for their conduct, which he says "*are best known to
themselves*," and without the knowledge of which,
nothing but the greatest confidence could have
prompted him to *suppose* an *address*, and to *expect*
an *answer*. But it is the eternal consequence of
ignorance united with *vanity*, that the former, seeing but little, is prompted by the latter to conceive,
not only, that it sees the whole; but that no others
see so much as he in whom they are conjoined.

That no evasion, no prevarication, no misrepresentation of the particulars contained in the preceding *address*, may be charged on me, I will examine every part of it, and give the whole a can-
did answer. The repeal of the stamp act was condemned because it was yielded to the demands of
Americans in rebellion, and because it tacitly allowed the parliament had no right to tax them. It sacri-
ficed the dignity of the legislature, and of the
executive power intrusted to those who were ministers when that repeal was passed. By the repeal of
the duties on glass, paper, and colours, still leaving that on tea existing, the purposes of supporting the sovereign authority, were kept as exec-
tive as if the other duties had not been repealed.
There was no risk, no danger, in the repeal; and
therefore nothing was ventured by the ministry,
which they had the least reason *not to venture*.

The pretence, as this gentleman stiles it, was,
that it was done "on the *true principles of commerce*, which shall be unanswerably proved when
I come to examine the letter of lord Hillborough.
The ministry were perfectly convinced that nothing
short of conceding not only all the taxes, but renouncing the supreme power of the realm would

sa-

satisfy those rebels. They estimated their increase
of *insolence* not at a pin's value. They derided the
necessity, which he represents they would be under, of *giving up* all the rest. And they prepared
to subdue their insolence, by means of that executive power which the minister of this speaker
so timidly relinquished to traitors, and *they* resolved
to look those in the face from before whom he fled,

Hence it appears, that "the objection was not
as good for preserving the five duties as for retaining the sixth." The repeal of the stamp act and of
the five duties have nothing analogous in their motives nor their consequences. And therefore the
" ill policy of the former, the mischiefs of which
were quite recent," was no small incentive to
avoid a repetition of that policy; and to avert the
like mischiefs of the last repeal. And now can it
be a presumption to say that on the principles of
Mr. Cornwall, and of the minister himself, *that*
minister had the ample means of answering the
supposititious address of your Orator?

Yet such is the confidence of this speaker, "he
pronounces that lord North "stands condemned by
" himself, and by all his associates, old and new, as
" a destroyer, in the first trust of finance, of the
" revenues; and in the first rank of honour, as a
" betrayer of the dignity of his country." Could
that minister be a destroyer of his financial trust by
repealing duties; that by the American prohibition of importing the commodities, on which they
were laid, into the colonies, had been rendered
impossible to produce a revenue? can that minister have betrayed the dignity of his country,
who hath so vigorously supported the sovereign
authority? can such a minister stand condemned
by himself and his associates, who hath thus conducted

ducted himself for the nation's welfare? but above all, is it not a stupendous act of confidence that this man, who prompted his master, to destroy the financial trust, by giving up the stamp duty; and to betray the dignity of his country by setting the legislative authority, like a broody goose on chalk eggs, to preserve the appearance of bringing forth, and yet to hatch nothing; that this man, who himself voted for both these indignities, confronted by the actual commission of those crimes which he so falsely imputes to lord North, should calumniate him as a *destroyer* of the *revenues*, and a *betrayer* of the *dignity of his country?* Surely his reason was fatigued, when he uttered these words; or all regard to truth, to decency, to his old master and himself had totally deserted him.

And now I will ask on whom the damnation of his proof is fallen? are the ministers with him? are they convinced that neither the repeal of the stamp act, nor any other, either had or could have the consequences which Mr. Cornwall imagined? does the conduct of the ministry give a conclusive answer to that gentleman's objection? is his proof irresistibly carried into the bodies of the ministry? are not all the circumstances he would destroy, like Falstaffe's buckram men, still alive and untouched?

However this confident calumniator of lord North is instantly become " his well-wisher," which it seems his lordship in common with other great men did not know. " he comes to rescue the noble lord " out of the hands of those he calls his friends, and " even out of his own." Ah what tenderness of heart does he possess! he is of a sensation so scrupulously delicate, that he cannot drown a kitten, in frosty

weather,

weather, unlefs it be in warm water. "He will
" do his lordſhip the juſtice he is denied at home.
. " He has not been this wicked or imprudent man.
" He knew that a repeal had no tendency to pro-
" duce the miſchiefs which gave ſo much alarm to
. " Mr. Cornwall. His work was not bad in its
" principle, but imperfect in its execution; and
" the motion on the paper preſſes him only to
" compleat a proper plan, which by ſome un-
" fortunate, unaccountable error, he had left un-
" finiſhed."

And now this miniſter "who, upon his own *principles*, in the preceding paragraph, had nothing to
anſwer; who ſtood condemned by himſelf and his
aſſociates, as a *deſtroyer* of the *revenues*, and a *betrayer* of the *dignity* of his *country*, is *not* this
wicked and imprudent man, his work was *not* bad
in its *principle*, but imperfect in its execution."
Such are the contradictions of which this orator
ſtands ſelf condemned. But let me not give him
and his aſſociates the occaſion of charging me with
not underſtanding his intention; and therefore of
miſrepreſenting him. In the preceding paſſage,
vanity, which never ſleeps in his boſom, prompted
him to believe that this *palinodia* would *ſoothe* the
miniſter to comply with that repeal for which he
was contending: and yet you have received repeated
proofs that nature has not intitled him, by her intellectual favours, to deem his talents to be ſo
ſuperior to thoſe of men, whom he oppoſes and de-
rides, as to afford him a rational confidence of
ſucceſs.

Such being the event of his damning proof,
he now "hopes Mr. Cornwal is thoroughly ſa-
" tisfied, and ſatisfied out of the proceeding of
" miniſtry on their own favourite act, that his
" fears,

" fears from a repeal are groundlefs." *Ignorance* then is the mother of *hope*, as fhe is faid to be of devotion. For on what other foundation can that hope be placed? and if Mr. Cornwal be fatisfied out of the proceedings of the minifter, he is the only man, who underftands the fubject, that can be thus fatisfied, and all his actions pronounce he is not that man.

However, " if *he* be not fatisfied, he leaves " him and the noble lord who fits by him to fettle " the matter as well as they can together; for if " the repeal of American taxes deftroys all our " government in America—he is the man!—and " he is the worft of all repealers, becaufe he is " the laft." This is certainly a new difcovery. For this *he* muft be Mr. Cornwal, or the paffage is nonfenfe, unlefs he fuppofes that thofe *two* make but *one be*: and yet till now it was underftood to be otherwife; that the minifter was the repealer. But whoever he be, I intreat you to mind his hypothetical reafoning, "*if* the repeal of Ame- " rican taxes deftroys all our government, he is " the worft of all repealers, becaufe he is the " laft."

But what act has lord North repealed, on which to ground this *if?* the duties on paper, glafs, and colours are indeed taken off by a fubfequent act, but is the act repealed which firft granted them, when it ftill remains in full force refpecting tea? if his lordfhip hath *repealed* that *act*, againft what does this fpeaker fo virulently *exclaim?* is not the effect produced, which he urges to obtain? has not lord North *perfected* the work which he charges him with having left *imperfect?* if he has not *repealed* it, how can he be deemed the worft of all *repealers* where no act is *repealed?* is it not impoffible to deter-
                                                                        mine

mine whether his imagination or his reason, his
inventions or his arguments be the more stupendous?

He presumes to be paramount in every human
faculty. And having so convincingly displayed his
reason and imagination, he now advances to shew
the amazing powers of his senses. " I *hear* it
" rung continually in my ears, *now* and *formerly*,
" says he, the preamble? what will become of the
" preamble if you repeal the tax?" What an as-
tonishing degree of perfection has nature given to
this sense! he hears *continually* that which is *past*,
and that which is *present*. His *now* includes them
both. It is a hearing devoutly to be wished. And
were he not so *over scrupulously delicate*, he might
with equal veracity affirm he *now* continually hears
what is to come. Nor is this sense more exquisite
than his others. *In like manner* he sees things both
out of sight and *in*; smells the *present* and the last
year's *rose*; tastes the venison of *this* and the *last*
season; and *now* touches, the salary which he has
not *fingered* these seven years. He exceeds *the most
wonderful wonder of wonders that ever was wonder-
ed at*.

But " the preamble! what will become of the
" preamble if the house repeal this tax." And
thus one of the American taxes, the *repeal* of which
made lord North, the worst of all the *repealers*, is
not repealed. " He is *sorry*, however, to be com-
" pelled so often to expose the calamities and dis-
" graces of parliament." Such sorrow it is as
Mark Antony expressed; when weeping over the
dead body of Cæsar he incensed the populace to
the destruction of Brutus, and of those who freed
their country from that tyrant; whose tyranny that
very Antony assisted in establishing.

" The

" The preamble of this law, he adds, has
" the lie direct given to it by the provisionary
" part of the act, if that can be called provisi-
" onary which makes no provision, nothing but
" truth could give him this firmness; but plain
" truth and clear evidence can be beat down by
" no ability." Let me examine into this *plain
truth* and *clear evidence.* The preamble says, "where-
" as it is expedient that a revenue should be raised
" in his majesty's dominions in America, for
" making a certain and adequate provision for de-
" fraying the charges of the administration of
" justice, and support of civil government, in
" such provinces where it shall be found necessary,
" and towards further defraying the expences of
" defending, protecting, and securing the said
" dominions." Such is the preamble, the provisionary part of the act imposes duties on tea,
glass, paper, and painter's colours, for the purposes abovementioned. And although the duties
be repealed on all but tea, in what manner, even
then can this provisionary part be said to make *no*
provision; or give the *lie direct* to the preamble,
when that duty still remains for further defraying
the preceding expences?

" You have heard," says he, in exultation,
" this pompous performance; now where is the
" revenue which is to do these mighty things? five
" sixths repealed—abandoned—sunk—gone—lost
" for ever." Hence it appears, through a want
of discernment, natural and frequent in this orator,
that he has mistaken the *act* that *repealed* the five
duties, by which they were sunk, &c. for that
which *imposed* them. And when he can prove that
these *two acts are one* and the same, then indeed,
and not till then, the provisionary part of that
which

which laid the duties will give the *lie direct* to its own preamble.

It is indeed in the power of legislature to make laws, but has it the power of making them obeyed but by coertion? when those duties were impo^ed, was it possible for adminiftration to fuggeft that the Americans could affume the impudence to interdict the importation of the commodities on which they were laid, and prefcribe laws to this kingdom refpecting what they fhould and fhould not export for the colonies, and thereby evade the intention of the Britifh legiflature? was it not, at that time as irreconcileable with that conftitutional authority which has conftantly impofed duties on imported goods, as it is, at prefent, that any man fhould defend their outrage, and pretend to love his country? but fuch being the event, the *revenue* was *gone before* the *repeal* of the five duties. And therefore *no revenue* could be abandoned, funk, gone, or loft for ever, by that repeal. He then afks, " does the poor folitary tea duty fupport the *pur-* " *pofe* of this preamble?" for raifing a revenue it does not; becaufe the duty has been never paid. But who, except this orator, is fo devoid of underftanding as not to be convinced that the duties, though exprefled for a revenue, were intended to be little more than the oftenfible reafons for that act; that the real object was the re-eftablifhment of the fupreme authority of the realm. Thofe taxes were therefore confidered as the means of carrying it into execution; and that end this poor folitary tea duty can as effectually obtain as the whole five, or fifty times that number could have done it. He perfifts, "it is not the fupply there ftated as " effectually abandoned as if the tea duty had " perifhed in the general wreck." if this orator,

when

when he was posting to Bristol, instead of being
robbed of *his* fourteen guineas, had been permitted to retain two pounds fourteen and eight-
pence of that money, would *his supply* have been as
totally taken away, as if he had been deprived of
all his guineas? and until he can prove, that five
parts in six make the *whole* of a thing, that supply
can never be as effectually abandoned, as if the
whole six had perished. But I confess this making
of *five* parts to be equal to *six* is attended with no
more difficulty than the dividing of *one* thing
into *three halves*. It shall soon be shewn you,
how this poor solitary tea is exalted into a matter
of the greatest concern to the commercial interest
of this nation.

" Here, Mr. Speaker," he *exclaims*, " is a pre-
" cious mockery, a preamble without an act."
And yet, in the preceding passage, he asserts that
this very act, which is *gone*, does *now* give the
lie direct to this preamble. " Taxes, says he,
" granted in order to be repealed; and the reasons
" of the grant still carefully kept up." Were
these taxes granted to be repealed? and are not
the reasons, the true and essential reasons, of the
grant still *carefully kept up*, by the preservation of
the duty on tea? this indeed is not at present:
" raising a revenue in America, but without its
" being kept up." None can be raised hereafter.
It would be in vain to expect obedience to the
parliament, after a second renunciation of all the
duties. The mischievous effects of the first flagitious dereliction of duty to their country, by
abrogating the stamp-act; the former incentives to
the present rebellion, irrefragably pronounce, that
a repeal of the tea tax would in fact be a sacrifice
of this kingdom to the colonies. It stands and is

as

as perfect a preservation of the dignity of England, as if every tax remained unabrogated.

In what then does "this precious mockery" consist; where is it so amply to be found as in the *act declaratory* of parliamentary right to tax America? a *right*, that by the whole tenor of this speech, as well as by other circumstances, it is expressly shewn, was never intended to be carried into execution. That was indeed a precious mockery! a vile delusion! an inhuman sacrifice of a nation's welfare to the private interest of a few pusillanimous individuals! "If you repeal this tax, "he continues, I readily admit that you lose this "fair preamble; estimate your loss in it; the "object of the act is gone already, and all you "suffer is the purging the statute book of the "opprobrium of an *empty*, absurd, and false re- ".cital." Such is the value at which he estimates that act which can alone sustain the dignity of this realm! such are the ignominious marks with which he brands it! The beauty of the figure, in which it is expressed, is perfectly adapted to the absurdity of the assertion: *purging* the statute book of the opprobrium of an *empty* recital *full* of absurdity and falsehood. Fertile as his imagination is said to be, by all those who conceive that incongruous images are proofs of a just fancy, he was not the original inventor of that thought. This *empty fullness* was the happy conception of an Irish merchant, who in an entry at a customhouse, among other things, inserted ten *empty* hogsheads *full* of salt water.

Mind how he advances in his progress. Having exhibited the accuracy of his reasoning, the justness of his imagination, and the acuteness of his senses, he now comes to manifest his commercial knowledge. "It has been said, again and again, "that

" that the five taxes were repealed on commercial
" principles ; it is so said in the paper in my hand;
" (lord Hilsborough's circular letter) a paper
" which I conftantly carry about, which I have
" often ufed, and fhall often ufe again." Does
he carry it about him as an *agnus dei*, a faint's
relique, to preferve him from injury ? or to what
ufe does he apply it? "what is got by this paultry
" pretence of commerce he knows not, for *if* your
" government in America is deftroyed by the *re-*
" *peal of taxes* ; it is of no confequence upon what
" ideas the repeal is grounded ; repeal this tax too
" upon commercial principles if you pleafe ; thefe
" principles will ferve as well now as they did
" formerly."

I agree with him indeed " *if* our government in
America be deftroyed by the *repeal of taxes*, it
is of no confequence upon what ideas the repeal
is grounded." But is it not of confequence
that our government be preferved by not repealing the tax on tea? and let me tell him that the
commercial principles on which the other duties
were repealed, will *not* ferve as well in the inftance
of tea, as in paper, glafs, red and white lead,
and painter's colours.

The firft principle of all commerce, is the employment of thofe who labour in our manufactures,
and other productions for exportation. And in proportion to the numbers employed will be the increafe of national opulence. When the Americans
refufed to receive into the colonies the manufactures of glafs, paper, and the other articles, it
was difcerned, by the minifter, that the diminution
of fale in thefe commodities would leffen the employment of thofe who worked in producing them.
In order therefore to obviate that evil, the taxes

on

on these were repealed, that the exportation might no longer be suspended. But tea employs no British subject either in its culture or preparation. The suspension of that export deprived no manufacturer of his employment. It was therefore reserved. And thus the repeal of the five duties was made on the first and truest of all commercial principles : and that on tea continued with that judgement which does honour to a minister. What then is the issue of this asseveration of this peremptory speaker, " that these commercial principles will serve as well to abrogate the duties on tea as on the other commodities?" such will inevitably be the event, when men presume to discuss all subjects who are well informed in none. Will he now persist in saying, "that the ministry " know, that their objection to a repeal, from " these consequences has no validity, or that this " pretence," as he calls it, " never could remove it."

Confident in all things, he asserts " this com- " mercial motive never was believed in America, " which this letter is meant to soothe, or in Eng- " land which it is meant to deceive." Thus he daringly presumes to answer for the belief of all America, and all England ; and yet it is nevertheless certain that every commercial man, in those dominions, who reflects one moment on this particular, must be convinced to demonstration, that such was the principle on which these duties were repealed. Notwithstanding this, he avers " it was " impossible it should, because every man the least " acquainted with the detail of commerce, must " know that several of the articles, on which the " tax was repealed, were fitter objects of duties " than almost any other articles that could possibly " be

" be chofen; without comparifon more fo than
" tea, that was left taxed, as infinitely lefs liable
" to be eluded by contraband." But I have already fhown you the motives on which thofe duties were repealed; and that he who is acquainted
with the leaft detail of trade muft know that the
duties were not repealed, becaufe the articles were
lefs liable to contraband than tea; but for reafons
which you have already heard. And you fhall foon
be convinced, that this tax on tea muft have proved
effectually preventive of contraband in that commodity, as well as the repeal muft be in fome of
the others. "You have, fays he, in this king-
" dom, an advantage in lead that amounts to a
" monopoly." In which *advantageous* monopoly,
and in one preparation of that metal, this orator
is poffeffed of a large fhare. It is in the making
of litharge; the *fcum* which rifes on the furface of
lead in *fufion*, and is rendered fo *light* as to be *blown*
from it by bellows, as faft as it is generated. By
the effects of this operation, that metal is changed
in colour; and affumes, among the vulgar, the
name of litharge of *gold*. Neverthelefs it is as
equally *lead* as before that procefs was performed.
Such is the nature of that metal, that, although
by art you may give it new colours, fhapes, and
confiftencies, it ftill remains in its fubftance abfolutely unchangeable; and is eafily reftored to its
genuine lumpifhnefs. This orator therefore being
fo great a monopolift, in this fcum of lead, is it
not natural for him to be a ftrenuous advocate in
fupporting the fale of that commodity?

" In all the articles of American contraband
" trade, fays he, who ever heard of the fmug-
" gling of red lead, and white lead?" who, indeed! it is a queftion proper to be afked only by

that

that connoiffeur in commerce, who ten lines before has told you that this kindom has a *monopoly*
in lead; and that it paid no duty either on export
or import. From whence then could it have poffibly been fmuggled? " fome of the things taxed,
" it feems, were fo trivial, that the objects them-
" felves, and their utter annihilation out of Ame-
" rican commerce, would have been comparative-
" ly as nothing." The *tax* therefore being of *lefs*
value than the *things themfelves*, muft be compara-
tively as *lefs* than *nothing*; and then this *non-exiftence*
would have been *annihilated* with the commodities;
which feems to be attended with fome difficulty in
the comprehenfion. " But is the article of tea
" fuch an object in the trade of England as not
" to be felt, or felt but flightly; like white lead,
" and red lead, and painter's colours? tea is an
" object of far other importance. Tea is per-
" haps the moft important object, taking it with
" its neceffary connections, of any in the mighty
" circle of our commerce. If commercial prin-
" ciples had been the true motives to this repeal,
" or had they been at all attended to, tea would
" have been the laft article we fhould have left
" taxed for a fubject of controverfy."

In his 14th page, he talks of the poor folitary
tea duty as unable to fupport the purpofes of
raifing a revenue. He tells you that five fixths of
the duties were abandoned, funk, gone, loft for
ever. It was to his purpofe then to leffen the confideration of tea, as I then remarked; and to exalt that of the other articles, as much as poffible.
But now he pipes another tune, " tea is perhaps
" the moft important object of any in the mighty
" circle of our commerce." And white lead, and
" red lead, and painter's colours, which would
" have

" have produced, as he says, three fifths of the
" five duties repealed, are reduced to objects not
" to be felt." Such is the confistency of this
mighty man of commerce. But then indeed he
says of tea, " taking it with its *neceffary* con-
"nections," by which it is manifest he has conceived
an idea that a *thing* may be taken, *without* that
with which it is *neceffarily connected*. It is his
peculiar excellence to conceive that impoffibilities
are practicable. But is *tea* with a *perhaps* and its
connections the most important object of our commerce? are the fugars which it caufes to be con-
fumed, the tea-kettles, and the china cups which
it employs, of more importance than the exportation of our woollen, our linnen, our iron,
or many other manufactures, when neither tea nor
China ware employ a fingle manufacturer of this
realm?

I have already fhewn you that the other duties
were repealed on motives of true commercial principles; that the tax on tea was left from *other* motives; and it fhall foon be evinced that the duty on
tea was the only one that ought to have been left,
when I examine his notions of contraband on
that particular.

You have now feen with what profundity of
judgement he is endued, refpecting commercial
matters. And now you fhall hear him reprehend and
reprobate the miniftry with as much arrogance and
licentioufnefs of tongue, as if the whole fyftem, not
only of commerce, but of all government, was in-
terwoven with the fabric of his foul. " It is not,
" fays he, a pleafant confideration, but nothing
" in the world can *read* fo awful and fo inftructive
" a leffon, as the *conduct* of miniftry in this bu-
" finefs, upon the mifchief of not having large

and

" and liberal ideas in this management of great
" affairs."

A *reading conduct*, how beautiful are the profo-
popœias with which his imagination furnishes you!
Such are the reprehenfions, fuch the obloquies
which are fo intrepidly pronounced by this fpeaker
whom you have already feen, without fufficient
intellect to comprehend that the firft principle of
commerce is to employ the people; that tea
being no manufacture of this realm, it was of lefs
moment whether it were received in America or
not; and that the manufacturing of wool, flax,
and iron, by which thoufands are fupported, are
of lefs importance than tea, which employs no
fingle fubject in its making. Even this man fo
tethered in his underftanding, arraigns " the conduct of the miniftry, and afcribes to them the
mifchief of not having *large* and *liberal* ideas in
the management of this great affair." I remember a blind man running againft a horfe that
ftood in the ftreet, who damned *it* for *not* being
able to *fee.*—But fuch is the misfortune of the
minifter, he cannot pleafe this exalted genius by
doing even what he approves. For he fays, " had
" the true motives to the repeal been attended to,
" tea would have been the *laft* article they fhould
" have *left* taxed for a fubject of controverfy."
This they have done. It is the *laft* tax that is *left*,
and *it is* the *fubject* of his *controverfy.* But you
fhall hear the whole of this antiminifterial *exclamation*, that you may draw a juft comparifon
between his prefumption and his knowledge.
" Never have the fervants of the ftate looked at
" the *whole* of your complicated interefts in one
" connected view." Is this an affertion too fcrupuloufly delicate from *one* who, to demonftration,

has

has not underftood one circumftance of that which
he criticifes and reviles? " they have taken things
" by bits and fcraps, fome at one time, and fome
" on one pretence, and fome at another, juft as
" they preffed, without any fort of regard to their
" relations or dependencies." Bravely pronounced
by one who, you are now convinced, does underftand neither *bit*, *fcrap*, nor *pretence*, of all the
affair he explodes. " They never had any kind
" of fyftem, right or wrong, but only invented
" occafionally fome miferable tale for the day, in
" order meanly to fneak out of difficulties, into
" which they had proudly ftrutted." Truth with
equal footfteps attends the progrefs of his affertions.
Their fyftem has been founded on juft principles;
and as uniformly purfued as the verfatility of political affairs can poffibly permit. It was begun
to awaken into action that fovereign power, which
this gentleman and his minifter had intentionally
lulled to eternal fleep, by the opium of their felf-
intereft. The duties on the commodities fo often
mentioned, were the means by which it was to be
exerted in America; when the Americans, with an
impudence, that no human forefight could divine,
refufed to admit thofe commodities into their
ports. The duties laid on the Britifh manufactures
were repealed, that the labour of the people and
the benefit of their fales might not be fufpended.
The tax on tea was continued to preferve the
fovereign authority in actual exercife. When the
merchants were intimidated from fending teas to
America, it was done by others, in order to prove,
by experiment, whether the Americans would dare
to prevent its importation. The populace grew
tumultuous on the arrival of the fhips; and committed felony by deftroying the tea. The ma-

giftrates abetted that outrage by a fcandalous in-
attention to their duty; and made no one attempt
to punifh fuch atrocious villains. In this ftate of
difobedience to the laws, and to the legiflative authority, it was demonftrable that nothing but force
could bring them to their duty, and troops were
fent as preparatory to that end : but that nothing of
cruelty might be juftly imputed to your fovereign,
his parliament, and his minifters, every merciful
attempt to bring them to obedience, and to fpare
the blood of thofe even, who by crimes had forfeited
their lives, was made. For thofe who feared no punifhment from judges equally rebellious with themfelves ;
and who by that fecurity were prompted to the com-
miffion of every outrage, a law was revived to obviate thofe ideas of illegal fafety, by which they
might be fent into England and be tried. At the
fame time, both exportation and importation, refpecting Bofton, was fufpended by parliament.
Such was the mercy of the legiflative power
of Britain, and fuch it remains, notwithftanding
their rebellion hath been fince that time aggra-
vated by deputies from the feveral colonies fuper-
feding the provincial legiflature, and affuming a
privilege to form a general congrefs, which hath
ufurped the rights, and renounced the fovereign
power of this kingdom. Even fince that time means
of fubmiffion have been propofed replete with clemency. Such is the origin, and fuch the progrefs
of that fyftem which this orator hath pronounced
to have no exiftence, and to be a miferable tale of
a day. And when he talked of *fneaking out of difficulties*, was it through want of reminifcence or
want of modefty that he pronounced thofe words fo
indifputably applicable to himfelf and his minifter.
  " They were, fays he, put to all thefe fhifts
" and devices, full of meannefs, and full of mif-
                                            " chief,

" chief, in order to pilfer, piece-meal, a repeal
" of an act, which they had not the generous
" courage, when they had found, and felt their
" error, honourably and fairly to difclaim." The
imputation of fhifts and devices, full of *meannefs*, and full of *mifchief*, the *pilfering*, as he dares
to call it, of an act piece-meal, have been fairly
difproved; but if the yielding to the claim of
rebels be a generous courage, and the furrender
of the Britifh fovereignty, an honourable and a fair
difclaimer, they have no fupport but in the egregious error, and mifchievous tranfgreffion committed by the Rockingham miniftry: a precedent,
too feeble to fuftain the defence of fo ruinous a timidity. And now, in order to exalt thefe hardy affertions by a figure equally bold to the knowledge they
include, he adds, " by fuch management, by the
" *irrefiftible* operation of *feeble* councils, fo *paultry*
" a fum as *three-pence* in the eyes of a financier,
" fo *infignificant* an article as *tea*, in the eyes of a
" philofopher, have fhaken the *pillars* of a com-
" mercial empire that circled the whole globe."
What a deal of mifchief this *three-penny* affair
has done! Ah! what an abominable " deftroyer
in the firft truft of the revenues muft this lord
North be, when, by his mal-adminiftration, fo
immenfe a fum is abandoned- funk—gone—
loft for ever!" Such an incomparable paffage
richly deferves a comment. 1. You are prefented
with the *irrefiftible ftrength* of *feeblenefs* that has *no*
ftrength at all. 2. That tea, which in the preceding page is the moft *important* object of the
Britifh commerce, is here reduced to a *three penny*
matter, in *finance*, and is become an object of *philofophy*, and 3. this *three pence* hath fhaken the pillars of a commercial *empire* that circled the globe.

The

The beauty of this metaphor is truly angelic, it is beyond human comprehenfion. The Britifh empire confifts of this kingdom, Ireland, a few ifles which lyè near them, Minorca and Gibraltar, in Europe; in Afia, of Bengal, part of the Carnatic and Bombay; in America, of the colonies, and feveral iflands. In what manner thefe places, which are fo many thoufand miles afunder, and lye in fuch different directions can form a circle, I am at a lofs to conceive. And, therefore, the new conception of pillars fupporting fuch portions of the earth can no more form a circle that furrounds the globe than the empire itfelf. But it has been faid, that the ocean forms a part of the Britifh empire. This, indeed, unites the parts of the *folid* empire, and encircles the globe. But an *ocean* fupported on pillars? how beautiful would it appear in painting! as the celebrated fpeakers of ancient and modern days, by *tropes* and *figures*, added wings to their orations that bore them into the fublimity of the fkies, fo does this fpeaker, of equal excellence in his kind, hang them on as weights to expedite his defcent into the immeafurable depths of the vaft *profound.* *

"Do you forget, fays he, that on the very laft "year you ftood on the precipice of general bank- "ruptcy? Your danger was, indeed, great; you "were diftreffed in the affairs of the Eaft India "company, and, you well know what fort of "things are involved in the comprehenfive ener- "gy of that fignificant appellation." That the Eaft India company were in fome danger of a bankruptcy two years fince; and that the government fupported them is well enough known. But that

---

* Bathos. chap. 10. the jargon.

that the nation was on the precipice of a bankruptcy can never be remembered, becaufe it did never
exift; and, therefore, it can never be forgotten, unlefs minifters have the fpecial gift of forgetting
what they never could have known. With what
unremitting ardor does he fupport the ftyle figurative ? The *involution* of things in the *comprehenfive* energy of a *word*, that fignifies the appellation
of the Eaft India company. If the Commons, or
Miniftry, do well know the *meaning* of thefe words,
I verily believe they know more than the orator
who fpoke them. I frankly confefs my ignorance.
However, it is an admirable expedient in a fpeaker,
who wants ideas, to *involve* his meaning in the
unintelligible *energy* of fonorous phrafeology.

He continues, " The monopoly of the moft
" lucrative trades, and the poffeffion of imperial
" revenues had brought the miniftry to the ve-
" ry verge of beggary and ruin. Such was their
" reprefentation – fuch, in fome meafure, was
" their cafe." From thefe words, you cannot but
infer that the miniftry are folely poffeffed of the
Eaft India trade; and that the Afiatic revenues are
received by them. Is the Eaft India company annihilated ? Could the miniftry reprefent that they
were brought to the very verge of beggary and
ruin ? Could that be, in fome meafure, the cafe
when they had nothing to do with the profits of
the trade, nor with the revenue, but that of re-
linquifhing the four hundred thoufand pounds a
year which the company was to pay them out of
a revenue of four millions? This fpeech appears to
be calculated for the Speakers in Leadenhall-ftreet;
and is manifeftly mifapplied in the houfe of Commons : " The vent of ten millions of pounds of
" this commodity, fays he, now locked up, by
" the

" the operation of an injudicious tax, and rotting
" in the warehouses of the company, would have
" prevented all this diftrefs, and all that feries of
" defperate meafures which the miniftry thought
" themfelves obliged to take in confequence of
" it." Here again, the three-penny matter of tea
is raifed to a two millions and a half of money,
the duty of which would be one hundred and
twenty-five thoufand pounds. For the firft fum,
at five fhillings per pound weight, on an average,
is its value; and the fecond the duty it would have
produced at three-pence a pound. Thus, the importance of this commodity finks and rifes occafionally; and the orator *, like a didapper, is either
above or under water, as it beft fuits his purpofe.

But let me examine a little into the merit of this
terrifying account of rotting tea. In page 36, he
tells you that the American confumption of teas is
annually 300,000 l. at the leaft farthing, by
which he *means worth* that fum. This if eftimated, at an average, of five fhillings the pound;
the quantity, which anfwers to the preceeding
fum of 300,000 l. will be annually 1,250,000
pounds weight; one-eighth of the ten millions.
Hence it refults, that there now lies rotting in the
warehoufes a quantity of tea equal to an eight years
fupply for America, accumulated by the Eaft-
India company in feven years, fix of which they
knew that the Americans would not receive it.
Thefe ten millions of tea, packed in the largeft
chefts and which therefore contain the greateft
quantity in the leaft fpace, would fill 30,000
chefts. If you enquire of a director where thefe

f   rot-

---

* Bathos. ch. 6. Didapper.

rotting millions of tea, and thoufands of chefts may
lie, he laughs in your face ; and affures you that
there is not an ounce of tea rotting, at this time,
more than ufual; and that neither the teas nor the
chefts are in their warehoufes. But fir, fays the
querift, the celebrated fpeaker Mr. Burke hath
afferted the firft, and confequently the fecond, in
parliament. Oh, I underftand you, fays he, they
are concealed with the army of prince Volfcius in
the inns at Knightfbridge.

Audacious as it may appear, I fhall venture to
affirm, that on the 19th of laft April, when this
fpeech was fpoken; and on the day when it was
printed alfo, there were not more than ten millions
of tea in the Eaft-India warehoufes, for the confumption of Great Britain, Ireland, the iflands ;
America ; and of all other places to which tea is
exported ; of which the colonies now in rebellion, do not confume more than a feventh part.
And as it is a well known truth, that the company
muft neceffarily have nearly a two years fupply of tea
conftantly in hand, by what means can ten millions
out of ten millions be now rotting in the India warehoufes, which would have been fent to America;
and yet a fufficient fupply remain for all the other
dominions of this realm ?

" America, however, would have furnifhed that
" vent, which *no* other part of the world can fur-
" nifh, *but* America;" that is *except* America.
And thus *America* and *itfelf* are two *different things*.
Unlefs the *fame thing* can be an *exception to itfelf*.
This admirable paffage exemplifies the *profundity*
of this gentleman's ftudies. He hath taken it from
that celebrated work in which he delighteth; and
in imitation of another *fhow-man*, who wrote over
the

the picture of his elephant, *this is the greateſt elephant in the world except himſelf.**

" Tea in America is next to a neceſſary of life ;
" and where the demand grows upon the ſupply."
This alſo is a new diſcovery in commerce, and
contrary to the opinion of all other men. For from
this obſervation it follows, the more there is of a
commodity at market, the greater is the demand for
it; and a ſupply is the more wanted. America therefore
can take not only all the tea that is brought to
England, but all that China can produce. Becauſe
the faſter the Americans are ſupplied, the more
they demand it. This I believe is a phœnomenon
ſo ſingular in the American commerce,
that although I am as convinced of the truth of
it as of any thing in Mr. Burke's oration; yet I am
told that the merchants are in ſome doubt, were
the import of tea open in America, whether it
would be prudent, notwithſtanding the reſpectableneſs
of Mr. Burke's opinion, to ſend tea to that
part of the world, if they heard there was a ſufficiency
for a year's conſumption.

He is conſtantly improving in the exhibitions
of his commercial learning ; " I hope, ſays he,
" our dear bought Eaſt-India committees have
" done at leaſt ſo much good as to let us know,
" that without a more extenſive ſale of that article,
" our Eaſt-India revenue and acquiſitions can have
" no certain connection with this country. It is
" through the American trade of tea, that your
" Eaſt-India conqueſts are to be prevented from
" cruſhing you with their burthen. They are
" ponderous indeed ; and they muſt have that
" great country to lean upon, or they tumble up-
                                                    " on

---

* Bathos. ch. 7. Of the profound when it conſiſts in the
thought.

" on your head." How *dearly* thefe committees
were bought, or *who paid* them I know not; but
this I know. It is a mortifying incident to a man,
to be left out in a *purchafe*, who has been ufed to
be included in thofe on Eaft-India fubjects.

In this inftance, this univerfal and comprehenfive
genius appears to be miftaken; not only in his notions of the Eaft-India trade, but in thofe of
geography alfo. Otherwife, can he fuppofe that
the revenues and acquifitions of Bengal and the
Carnatic can have no certain connection with this
country, but through the American trade of tea?
Do thefe provinces lie in China, and pay their revenues in that commodity? it has hitherto been
thought that the revenue is paid in filver in Bengal,
and thence carried to China to purchafe teas. And
could not that filver be brought to England but
through the American trade of tea? can the trade
of that tea to America, amounting only to a
feventh part of the annual fale, prevent this kingdom from being crufhed by the burthen of our
Eaft-India conquefts? but the metaphor is admirable beyond comparifon. "Thofe ponderous
conquefts in Afia muft have the great country
of America to *lean* upon, or they tumble upon
your heads." If you underftand *lean* as a *trope*
to exprefs *lie*, then he has fuppofed thefe Afiatic
conquefts muft be carried, by fea I prefume, fome
thoufand leagues, and placed on the colonies in
America, where they will lie, one upon another,
like pancakes in a difh. And then our heads will
be effectually fecured from being tumbled on; and
ourfelves from being crufhed by their burthen.
If by the word *lean*, he means to give perfonality
to our Indian conquefts, then he muft fuppofe
that, by *leaning* on the provinces of America, per-

fonified

fonified alſo, they will be prevented from falling on our heads in England, which is certainly a fact; for if they *lean* there, ſhould their props fail them, they can never *fall* here, be they as ponderous as they may.

"It is the ſame folly that has loſt you the be-"nefit of the Weſt, and of the Eaſt," ſays he, "this folly has thrown open folding doors to con-"traband, and will be the means of giving the "profits of the trade of your colonies to every "nation but yourſelves." I appeal to experience for the falſity of having loſt the benefit of our eaſtern trade. And if the Americans are not reduced to obedience, I will allow him that of the Weſt. But nothing in contention can be loſt until the conteſt be decided. And does he conceive the Americans can defeat our troops; the provinces become ſeparate ſtates; and in ſpite of our fleets trade with other nations? but you ſhall ſoon be ſhown that his knowledge of the contraband trade in America, is equal to that which he has exhibited reſpecting that of Aſia. He continues to *exclaim* "never did a people ſuffer ſo much for the empty "words of a preamble. It muſt be given up." I wiſh the orator had explained in what theſe ſufferings conſiſt. Not in the loſs of the Eaſt-India trade it is ſelf-evident; and the preſent interruption to that with the provinces hath hitherto been the parent of very little ſufferings. We have ſeen an application from Birmingham, and another from the clothiers in the Weſt of England, approving the conduct of the miniſters, and petitioning for a continuance of their attempts to ſubdue the refractory ſpirit of rebellion in America. We have ſeen from Leeds in Yorkſhire, in contradiction to a letter promulged by a quaker, that the decline

of

of trade was not more, at that time, than usual. All these are places of manufacturing as considerable as any in England. Is it natural for men to suffer, and to petition for the continuation of those measures by which they are oppressed? where then are your sufferings? but alas! such must be your fate, for according to this speaker it is irremediable. I presume the *words* of the preamble make the preamble itself. If the words be *empty*, they have no *meaning*. How then can a preamble that means *nothing* be given up? have you, till this time ever heard of a *surrender of nothing at all?* he then asks, "on what principle does it stand?" indeed I never could have answered this question because I have never conceived that *emptiness* could stand upon *any thing*. Happily, and according to his usual benignity he answers himself. "This "famous revenue stands, at this hour, *on all the* "*debate*, as a description of a revenue not as yet "known in all the comprehensive (but too com- "prehensive) vocabulary of finance—*a preambu-* "*lary tax*." Hence it is plain, that the *empty* preamble is synonimous with the revenue, or *pre- ambulary tax*. And thus this tax, which *walks before itself*, does nevertheless *stand* as a revenue *on all the debate*. And thus the *debate* is the principle on which it *stands*. But it seems nevertheless that this *preambulatory* tax does not stand as a revenue on its *principle* the *debate*, but as a *description* of revenue not yet known in the vocabulary of finance. The *description* is its *locum tenens*. And yet it is a *description unknown* in all the too comprehensive vocabulary of finance. A *word book* of finance is a new production. It is indeed as singular as this speech, it is *too com-*

comprehensive, and yet it does not *comprehend* the *description* which ought to be in it.* May not this notion of a *description* standing as a *locum tenens* in place of a reality be usefully applicable by the lord mayor and aldermen of London? for example, may not the former send his pourtrait or statue in brass as a *thing* to supply the absence of himself, and the presence of an alderman, and all things proceed as well as if both of them were present? Surely such unintelligible and contradictory circumlocution was never heard before this exhibition of our orator. But let me risk a presumption to understand his intent, and suppose the whole of this pompous periphrase to signify that the tax is in the preamble, and such as was not known before. He hath already told you of what this preamble consists, " that it is expedient " that a revenue should be raised in America for " making a more certain provision for defraying " the charge of the administration, of justice, " the support-of-civil government, and towards " defending, protecting, and securing the said " dominions."

Do you find this tax in the *preamble?* the preamble declares for what ends it was to be raised, and no more. And from that alone it is impossible to learn what tax is. Unless Mr. Burke *can see at Cannon what was never there*, and find something

---

* Bathos. ch. 11. *Macrology* and *pleonasm* are as generally coupled as a lean with a fat rabbit; nor is it a wonder the superfluity of words and vacuity or sense being just the same thing. ch. 12. The expression is adequate when it is proportionably low to the profundity of the thought. It must not be always grammatical, lest it appear pedantic and ungentlemanly: nor too clear for fear it become vulgar: for obscurity bestows a cast of the wonderful, and throws an oracular dignity on a piece that hath no meaning.

thing *in* a box which it does *not contain*. The tax
in this, as in all other acts, is in the body of the
statute ; and this preamble, which contains the *description* of a revenue that is *not* described, like
all other preambles, declares the purposes for which
the tax is to be levied. And surely such a preamble is not unknown to the nation; although it may
be wanting in the *too comprehensive* vocabulary of
this speaker's financial knowledge.

Mark how he kindles, like the axle of a loaded
cart, from ponderosity and friction. How beau-
tifully he amplifies on this *preambulary tax.* "It
" is indeed a tax of sophistry, a tax of pedantry,
" a tax of disputation, a tax of war and rebellion,
" a tax for any thing but benefit to the imposers,
" or satisfaction to the subject." If you adhere
to the grammatical meaning of these words, this
tax is a taxation of *sophistry*, of *pedantry*, of *disputation*, of *war* and *rebellion*; and then envy
must confess that this gentleman is fully justified
in *exclaiming* so violently against that tax to which
he must be so great a contributor. But then the
word *tea* must be synonimous with all *these*, which
I believe does not appear in the vocabulary of
finance. The preceding passage will however gram-
matically admit another sense ; that this tea duty
was imposed by *sophistry*, *pedantry*, *disputation*,
war, and *rebellion*. And then the speakers, at
least, if not all who voted for this tax, are con-
sequently *sophistical*, *pedantic*, *disputatious*, *war-
like*, *rebellious* subjects. But as it is the indigenous
and innate right of this speaker, to say one thing
and to mean another; as his heritage is large, and
he bestows it with the genuine spirit of true—Irish
hospitality; as he has a just claim to that right also
by the parliamentary precedent of dividing a sub-

E   ject

ject into three halves ; perhaps he may mean that
this tax *hath been productive* of *fophiftry, pedantry,
difputation, war,* and *rebellion.*— It has indeed
been productive of fophiftry, pedantry, and difputation, to the proof of which I fubpœna no
evidence but this fpeech. As to war and rebellion, thofe were produced by fpeeches in parliament, in oppofition to the ftamp-act, and
foftered by the repeal of it. However, to be
partly right, is fo much a novelty in this fpeaker ;
that I intreat you to place the merit of it to his
account.

" Well, fays he, but whatever it is gentlemen
" will force the colonies to take the tea, you will
" force them? has feven years ftruggle been able
" to force them? oh! but it feems we are in the
" right, the tax is trifling---in effect it is rather an
" exoneration than an impofition, three fourths of
" the duty formerly payable on teas exported to
" America is taken off; the place of collection is
" only fhifted ; inftead of the retention of a fhil-
" ling from the draw-back here, it is three-pence
" cuftom paid in America. All this is very
" true, but this is the very folly and mifchief of
" the act. Incredible as it may feem, the mi-
" niftry know that they have deliberately thrown
" away a large duty which they held fecure and
" quiet in their hands, for the vain hope of get-
" ting one three fourths lefs, through every ha-
" zard, through certain litigation, and poffibly
" through war."

I fhall not examine any farther into the folly
and mifchief of the act, it has been already evinced
that the true motive to enacting it was the
reviving of the fovereign authority of Britain in
America; that the revenue was the oftenfible
reafon,

reafon, and the means of exerting that fupreme
power. But without having recourfe to thofe particulars, I will examine it as a revenue act alone.
Before the time of its being paffed, every pound
of tea, that was exported to America, went from
England one fhilling dearer, than after the act was
made. This fhilling was taken off, and on the teas
being landed in America they paid three-pence per
pound weight. Teas that, fince the alteration,
may be exported at half a crown a pound. were,
before it, with the fhilling, at the price of three
and fix-pence. The fame teas, with the three-pence
duty, are now worth two fhillings and nine-pence
in the colonies. The Americans paying the former
fhilling duty in the price, paid forty per cent. on
the teas of two and fix-pence per pound. They
now pay ten. And as the teas exported increafed
in prime coft, this fhilling gradually decreafed
from forty to ten per cent. on teas between half a
crown and ten fhillings a pound. At prefent with
the duty of three-pence, they decreafe from ten
to two and a half per cent. The profits, by evading
the payment of the fhilling, or forty per cent. on
thofe teas which are chiefly demanded in America,
as well as the evafion of the proportion of it in
teas of all prices, were an incentive to fmuggling
too ftrong to be refifted ; and the contraband in
that article being confequently very great on that
account, the export of tea from England to the
colonies was vaftly inferior to the confumption of
it in America. Adminiftration therefore on the
eftablifhed and true principles of trade and finance,
concluded that three-pence per pound, on all teas,
would render the fmuggling of them fo little advantageous, that it would be no longer purfued.
And confequently that the fmall duty, by increafe

of

of sale, would more than compensate for that of
the large that was taken away. The tax therefore
is indeed both trifling, and an exoneration. But
where is the folly, where the mischief that has been
done by the ministry, in thus diminishing this tax?
how have the ministry deliberately thrown away a
large duty, which they held in their hands, for the
vain hope of getting three fourths less. Does it
not, as this speaker says, seem incredible, that he
should be so definitive and peremptory in the reprehension of that which he so little understands?
the ministry indeed might easily foresee that the
principles which had been propagated by the American advocates in parliament, might create litigation; but could they believe that the colonies would dare to oppose a tax on importation,
which had been the usual and undisturbed practice
from the time of king William to the day on
which that tax was imposed? At least they resolved to restore the sovereign power, which had
been abandoned, through every hazard, even to
war; *they* have the dignity of their country at
heart, and *they* will not timidly yield to the demands of rebellion.

The folly and mischief imputed to the ministry,
may now seem to be transferred to him that pronounced it, of which a further confirmation will
arise from the following assertion. " The manner of
" proceeding in the duties on paper and glass, im-
" posed by the same act, was exactly in the same
" spirit. There are heavy excises on those arti-
" cles, when used in England. On export, these
" excises are drawn back; but instead of with-
" holding the draw-back, which might have been
" done, without possibility of smuggling; and
" instead of applying the money (money already
" in

"in their hands) according to their pleasure, they
"began their operations in finance, by flinging
"away the revenue; they allowed the whole
"draw-back on export., and then they charged
"the duty (which they had before discharged) pay-
"able in the colonies, where it is certain the col-
"lection would devour it to the bone, if any
"revenue were ever suffered to be collected.
"One spirit pervades and animates the whole
"mass."

This opinion of our orator in this instance is
exactly in the same spirit of commercial knowledge with the preceding. He tells you there are
heavy excises on paper and glass, which on export
are drawn back; that these might have been withheld with ease by the ministry, and that they begun with flinging away a revenue in their hands,
when he has this moment told you that no such revenue existed, the excises being drawn back on
exportation. However his meaning is that the
withholding of heavy excises in England, on
glass and paper, which must be paid by the colonists in the price of them, is a more judicious
mode than laying a small tax on them, to be paid
in America. And this he says might have been done
without a possibility of smuggling. That the desire
of evading the payment of these *heavy excises* on the
preceding commodities, would naturally excite the
practice of contraband, he will hardly deny. But
it seems such an illicit trade is impossible. Yet paper
and German glass are to be exported from Holland
at a much less price than they are from England,
after the draw-back is allowed. St. Eustatia and
Curasoe are Dutch islands, from whence a variety
of merchandise is smuggled into America. Had
the *heavy excises* been retained in England, when

E 3

these

thefe commodities were exported to America, would not that aggravation of price have proved to be an incitement to finuggling, and have overcome this orator's *impoffibility*; have thrown open folding-doors to contraband; and inftead of enabling the miniftry to keep thofe excifes, as a revenue in the hands of government, would it not have annihilated the American fale of the commodities on which they were laid; and have transferred that money, which before came here, into the Dutch dominions? even the fmall duty, impofed on thefe commodities, when imported into America, manifeftly tending to promote a contraband, was one among the commercial motives that induced the prefent miniftry to repeal thofe duties. Where now is the folly to be placed? but it appears that this gentleman's ideas of contraband are, that the greater the *profits* of *fmuggling*, the *lefs* will be the *incitement* to contraband. Is he not always miftaking the hatchet for the helve, and cutting his fingers by handling what he does not underftand? *does not one fpirit pervade and animate his whole mafs?*

" Could any thing, fays he, be a fubject of
" more juft alarm to America, than to fee the
" miniftry go out of the plain high road of fi-
" nances, and give up the moft certain revenues
" and the cleareft interefts, merely for the fake of
" infulting the colonies?" but fuch is the truth that *lowering* the duty on *tea*, and not impofing duties on things which other nations can more cheaply fupply, are the certain ways of increafing a revenue, and the interefts of a nation. And would it not, on that account, have been going out of the plain road of finance, to have withheld the excifes which had been conftantly drawn back

on

on export ? and in what manner were the colonifts
infulted by the exercife of that power, of laying
duties on American imports, which had been in
continual ufage fince the day on which the Bofto-
nians received their charter from William the
third ? even that authority which this gentleman's
minifter produced a declaratory act to juftify and
eftablifh ; which *he* advifed, and on the rectitude
of which *he* fpoke. "No man, fays he, ever
" doubted that the commodity of tea could bear
" an impofition of three-pence." Then why does
he *exclaim* againft the miniftry who impofed it?
but he adds " no commodity will bear three-pence,
" or will bear a penny, when the general feelings
" of men are irritated, and two millions of people
" are refolved not to pay." I fhould imagine,
unlefs the commodity had feelings like the people,
it might bear it well enough. But I conclude that
he means, if two millions of men are irritated,
and are refolved *not* to pay, why then they will
not pay. And therefore, as the law directs, and
the duty of adminiftration requires, they muft be
compelled to it by the executive power. For if no
taxes were paid, but fuch as men would be willing
to pay, I fancy the government would have but a
fcanty revenue.

"The feelings of the colonies were formerly
" the feelings of Great-Britain." It is indifputably
true, that when the colonies were diftreffed, Great
Britain hath always *felt* for them ; witnefs the
feventy millions fhe ran in debt to fupport them
in the laft war ; witnefs the numbers of Britons
that perifhed in her caufe ; witnefs the ready attention fhe hath ever paid to all things that might
promote their intereft. But the *feelings* of *Great
Britain* have *not* been thofe of the *colonies*, for with

E 4   the

the immenfe advantages which they acquired by
the peace, the traiterous ingrates now refule conftitutionally to contribute to the fupport of their
own governments.

The gentleman having thus exhibited unparalleled proofs how perfectly he is inftructed in
the fubject of commerce, takes an occafion to
difplay his knowledge in the hiftory of *this* country. " Theirs were formerly the feelings of Mr.
" Hampden, when called upon for the payment of
" twenty fhillings. Would twenty fhillings have
" ruined Mr. Hampden's fortune? no! but the
" payment of twenty fhillings, on the principle
" it was paid, would have made him a flave. It
" is the weight of that preamble, of which you
" are fo fond, and not the weight of the duty
" that the Americans are unable and unwilling to
" bear,"

Let me examine into this identity of feelings in
Mr. Hampden and the Americans. Charles the
firft and his minifters, by an exertion of the prerogative royal, commanded his officers to collect the
tax of fhip money. Mr. Hampden infifted that the
king had no right to raife money in that manner;
becaufe none but the fovereign authority of parliament could impofe a duty on the fubjects of
England. And therefore the proclamation of the
king being illegal and arbitrary, he would not
comply with that demand.

The parliament of this realm have enacted a
tax to be paid by the American fubjects. Thefe
Americans refufe to obey the law becaufe, as they
aver, by the charters of former kings, they are
exempted from paying any tax but what they impofe on themfelves. In Great Britain, none but
the parliament can legally levy a tax, and every
exertion

exertion of that kind in a fovereign is tyranny,
In America, none but the king can impart the
right of impofing a duty, and it is tyranny in the
legiflative power of this realm to levy it. Mr.
Hampden, in obeying the king's prerogative,
would have been a flave, and free under a parliamentary taxation in England. The Americans
are flaves if they obey the parliament, and free
under the prerogative royal. Thus the conftitution
of this realm is made to conform to the different
inclinations of the fubjects, as foxes in the moft
northern climates change colour according to the
feafons. For if the king, by charter, can grant
the right of impofing taxes, to his American fubjects, and thereby free them from the obligation
of being obedient to the acts of the Britifh legiflature, then is he fuperior to himfelf and his
parliament; and the tax of fhip money was no illegal demand. For certainly he that can juftly annihilate the parliamentary power over his fubjects
in America, can raife a tax in this kingdom without their confent. But you all know that a Britifh
fovereign has no right to tax you by his prerogative ; and therefore he can never transfer, by
charter, to the Americans, that *right* which he
does *not* poffefs, *an exemption from being taxed by a
Britifh parliament*. This truth is evinced by every
charter that has been granted to the cities and towns
of England, and even to the colonies themfelves.
Every law they make, repugnant to the laws of
England is exprefsly null and void? can they
therefore be poffeffed of a right to make laws, and
not to apply them? does not the fame power
which annihilates fuch laws, abfolutely pronounce
that they can have no right to make them ? they
have all a right to raife on themfelves what money
they

they pleafe for their own ufe ; yet are they neverthelefs as much obliged to pay the taxes of the
ftate as thofe who are not incorporated by charters.
Such is precifely the cafe of the colonies and of all
other corporations?

What ideas then does our orator entertain of
the identity, or even fimilitude of feelings, between
Hampden and the colonifts? can the fame feelings
arife from caufes fo irreconcileably contradictory?
are the equator and the meridian circles lefs parallel than thefe cafes of Hampden and the colonifts? what motive could have led him to il-
luftrate his fubject by an inftance which in every
point directly oppofes what he intended to eftablifh? this is indeed " *underpinning with clumfy but-*
" *tereffes a pillar which they overthrow.*" And thus
you fee his fkill in reafoning by analogy is equal
to his logical induction, and his knowledge of hiftory to that of commerce. And now you may
talk as you will of the mulberry tree, commend
me to a bit of fhillalah.*

However " it is the weight of the preamble,
" and not the weight of the duty that the Ame-
" ricans are unable and unwilling to bear." They
can bear the *tax*, but *will not bear* the *weight* of
the preamble. This weight confifts in the raifing
a revenue in fupport of the adminiftration of
juftice, of the civil government, and for defending, protecting, and fecuring themfelves and their
properties. This it feems they *can* and ought to
bear, and *will not*. This alfo is indeed a new method of defence by bringing proof to the contrary of what he intended. Thefe Americans who
trumpet their loyalty fo loudly in all their rebellious

---

* Irifhman in the *Jubilee.*

ous publications, it seems *can* but *will not* contribute to the support of *themselves*. You and I and all the subjects of Great Britain and Ireland are not only to discharge the interest of seventy millions, borrowed to save them from destruction in the last war, but to support them for the future without their contributing but what they please to their own preservation, both in civil and military departments. *They* are to be exempted from the controul of the legislature, and *you* obliged to obey it. *They* are to be *free* from *imposts*, and *you* to be unremittingly *oppressed* for *them*. In fact, they are to be your *masters*, and you their *slaves*. *They* are to wanton in ease and voluptuousness, and *you* to labour for the supporting of them. Such are the purposes which this orator and his confederates are labouring to establish. And under the delusive terms of supporting *liberty* in *America*, actually to *enslave* you in *England*. Will you, descended from ancestors who disdained to be enthralled by *sovereigns*, submit to the bondage of *men* generated from those who were either by principle and by practice enemies to your constitution ; or from *such*, as having forfeited their lives by felony, in this kingdom, were transported to the colonies ? it cannot be ! " It is, says he, upon the *principle*
" of this measure, and nothing else, that we are
" at issue; it is a principle of political expen-
" diency." It is indeed the expediency of re-
establishing the legislative authority in America,
so industriously concealed from you through his
long harangue. " The act of 1767 asserts that it
" is expedient to raise a revenue in America; the
" act of 1769, which takes away that revenue,
" contradicts the act of 1767, and by something
" much stronger than words, asserts, that it is not
" ex-

" expedient." The former act asserts it is *expedient*, that is *fit, proper*, to raise a revenue; the
taxes were the means by which it was to be raised.
The act of 1769 repeals five of these duties, for commercial reasons already assigned. The tax on tea
still remains. Now in what sense can the *repeal* of
duties *contradict* the *fitness* and *properness* of raising
a revenue? the repeal brings no proof, but that
the means were improper for the end, and therefore repealed. But the expendiency, the fitness of
raising a revenue subsists as much before as after.
Is it not expedient, that all artisans should live by
their labour, but if by any incident or design,
their employment be taken from them, does that
event contradict the expediency, the fitness, the
properness, that these men should live by their
labour? I am apprehensive then that this orator
either does not understand the word *expedient*, or
that he draws a conclusion which is the reverse of
logical induction, like a Welch groom that curries
the horse from the *head* to the *tail*, and then wipes
him backwards from the *tail* to the *head*.

He comes now to arraign the wisdom of parliament. " It is a reflection upon your wisdom to
" persist in a solemn parliamentary declaration of
" the expediency of any object, for which, at the
" same time you make no provision." Surely the
gentleman has not exhibited much wisdom in this
assertion. Whilst the Americans are in rebellion,
and will submit to no law made in England, can
it be a *reflection* on the wisdom of parliament that
they make *no* provision, when it is certain, that
none can be made? is it a *reflection* on their wisdom
to persist in the declaration of their *fitness* of an
object which *ought* to be obtained? if by any
means the usual supply of provisions for the city

of London should be withheld by Bakers, Brewers, Butchers, &c. would it be a reflection on the wisdom of parliament to declare the *expediency* of the several objects for supporting life, because the men above-mentioned would not bring their commodities to market? would not parliament behave, in that case, as they do in the present, compel those fellows to supply the markets; or permit the people to take the provisions without their consent? has this *speaker* been so conversant in Ecclesiastes and the books of Solomon, that he can, with justice, so confidently reprehend the *wisdom* of parliament?

He now intreats the Commons to attend with more particular care. " Pray, let not this cir-
" cumstance escape you; it is very material; that
" the preamble of this act, which he wishes to
" repeal, is not *declaratory of a right*, as some
" gentlemen seem to argue it; it is only a recital
" of the *expediency* of a certain exercise of a right,
" supposed already to have been asserted; an ex-
" ercise they are now contending for by ways and
" means, which they confess, though they were
" obeyed, to be utterly insufficient for their pur-
" pose." Can it be material to tell the house, that an act, which was *never* intended to be *declaratory*, is *not* that which it was *not* intended to be; because some gentlemen *seem* to think so? This preamble, which he has already declared to contain a revenue, a description of a revenue, a tax of sophistry, pedantry, disputation, war and rebellion, which must be given up, "is now *only* a recital
" of an expediency of a certain exercise of a right
" supposed already to have been asserted." And thus he confesses, that this preamble does contain a recital of the expediency of exercising
the

the legiſlative authority of this realm. Is it a right
ſuppoſed to have been aſſerted, when the records
of parliament *pronounce* it *has been exerted* from
the revolution to that act to which he refers? A
right *ſuppoſed*, after *his* maſter had obtained, and
he had voted for an *act declaratory* of that very
right. As to the confeſſion of the commons, or
the miniſtry, that if the " ways and means for
" which they are contending were obeyed, they
" would be utterly inſufficient." As he quotes
no ſuch confeſſion, I ſhall ſuſpend my belief. For
it has been ſufficiently evinced that this orator is
capable of miſtakes. And now for the concluſion
from his premiſes, " you are therefore at this
" moment in the awkward ſituation of fighting
" for a phantom, a quiddity; a thing that wants
" not only a ſubſtance, but even a name; for a
" thing which is neither abſtract, right, nor pro-
" ſitable enjoyment." Such is this gentleman's
idea of the ſovereign legiſlative power of this
kingdom. And now it reſults, that this terrible
preamble, which muſt be repealed, becauſe it
contained the tea duty, does really contain nothing
at all, neither *name* nor *ſubſtance*. I wiſh he had
inſtructed the houſe in the manner of repealing
nothing at all; the file affords no precedent. And
thus from his own lips it appears that theſe miniſters, who are ſo extremely criminal, in not
having repealed this preamble, have *nothing* to repeal; and that this orator hath been haranguing
upon *nothing at all* through ſuch a prolix pro-
fuſion of verboſity. Thus the matter ſo *material*, the eſcape of which the houſe was prayed
not to permit, ends in quips and quiddities, phan-
toms, and things without name or ſubſtance; and
then what need was there of adding, that a *nothing*
was

was neither abstract, right, nor profitable enjoyment ?

"They tell you, says he, that your dignity is
" tied to it, but he knows not how it happens,
" but this dignity is a terrible incumbrance to
" you; for it has of late been ever at war with
" your interest, your equity, and every idea of
" your policy. Shew the thing you contend for
" to be reason; shew it to be common sense;
" shew it to be the means of attaining some useful
" end; and then he is content to allow it what
" dignity you please. But what dignity is derived
" from the perseverance in absurdity is more than
" ever he could discern." This challenge I shall
presume to answer, and to shew the thing con-
tended for, to be *reason*, *common sense*, and to attain some *useful end*. Is not the support of the
sovereign authority of this realm an object of dignity? is it not the interest of the whole nation
that it should be supported? Is it not equitable
that the Americans should obey this power, and
contribute to the supplies of money which are requisite for administering justice and defending
themselves? are these things at war with every idea
of British policy? how then is this *dignity* at war
with the preceding things? is it not therefore shewn
that it is both reason, common sense, and to the
attainment of some useful end? let him therefore
prove that these particulars are otherwise, or allow
them that dignity which they truly deserve. However, that he cannot discern what *dignity* is derived
from the perseverance in absurdity, I do verily
believe; for if he had possessed that talent, this
speech would neither have been spoken nor printed.

It must be confessed, however, that what he wants
either in candour and discernment, is amply compenfated

penfated by his confidence. For in plain Englifh, the preceding paffage expreffes nothing lefs than, that the commons are a pack of fellows fo ignorant they know not their *own intereft*, their *own equity*, nor have they *one idea* of their *own policy*. That they are contending for what has neither *reafon* nor *common fenfe*, nor *one ufeful end*; and that their whole conduct is a *perfeverance in abfurdity*. It muft be remarked that this becoming paffage was fpoken of the laft parliament. Of the prefent, he has not printed his opinion.

He then tells you, that " Mr. Cornwal has faid
" that this fubject does not ftand now as it did
" formerly. Oh! certainly not; every hour they
" continue on this ill-chofen ground, their diffi-
" culties thicken on them; and therefore his con-
" clufion is, remove from a bad pofition as quickly
" as you can, the difgrace and the neceffity of
" yielding, both of them grow upon them every
" hour of their delay." This reminds me of the fon of Æolus, whom his father inftructed in the fecret of inclofing the winds in leathern bottles, which he was to fell to thofe who might want his commodity. But as he had but little demand for his merchandife in the ifland in which he was born, near Great Britain, he travelled to Bætica; in which kingdom wealth abounded, in hopes of felling his *wind* for fubftantial riches. His method was to perfuade them to refign their gold, and to rely on their imaginations for being enriched by him. In this perfuafion he diftributed a large part of his *wind*. They at length believed; and were thereby deprived of three parts in four of their wealth. Such was the *windy* influence of the fon of Æolus. Perhaps a fimilar intention might have engaged our orator to part with his *wind*, in order

to

to delude the parliament and the minifters from their undertakings, refpecting America. He is underftood as delivering the fubfequent words. Commons and minifters follow the example which was fet you by my minifter, and by my advice; repeal the duty on tea, as the ftamp-act was abrogated, in obedience to the rebellious demands of the Americans; facrifice the rights of parliament; difhonour the king's dignity; betray the truft of adminiftration which is repofed in you; fet the Americans in an independency of the legiflature, and free from taxation; and continue to opprefs the fubjects of England by new impofts on their account. Otherwife your difficulties will thicken upon you, your difgrace and the neceffity of yielding will grow upon you every hour. But neither the commons nor the miniftry were otherwife moved by his *wind*, than to deride the propofal. They faw the inclination and the ends which urged him to the attempt of bringing *them* to a repetition of the follies above recited. But they difcerned not the defire of yielding to the Americans, nor the difgrace of defending all that dignity which the Rockingham miniftry fo timidly refigned.

He continues, " but will you repeal the act, " fays Mr. Cornwall, at this inftant, when Ame- " rica is in open refiftance? he thinks he has " driven them into a corner; but thus pent up, " he is content to meet him, becaufe he enters the " lifts fupported by his old authority, Mr. Corn- " wall's new friends, the miniftry themfelves." It is indeed an heroic act of chivalry. This oratoric champion, pent up in a corner, fupported by the miniftry, Mr. Cornwall's new friends, is content to meet that gentleman, who, if that be

true,

true, has no one to affift him. You fhall hear the
defence he makes. " Mr. Cornwall remembers
" that about five years ago, as great difturbances,
" as the prefent, prevailed in America, on ac-
" count of the new taxes. The miniftry repre-
" fented thefe difturbances as treafonable; and
" this houfe, thought proper, on that repre-
" fentation, to make a famous addrefs for a re-
" vival, and for a new application of a ftatute of
" Henry VIII. The commons befought the king,
" in that well confidered addrefs, to enquire into
" treafons; and to bring the fuppofed traitors
" from America to Great Britain for trial. His
" majefty was pleafed gracioufly to promife a
" compliance with their requeft. All the at-
" tempts from this fide of the houfe, to refift
" thofe violences, and to bring about a repeal,
" were treated with the utmoft fcorn. An ap-
" prehenfion of the very confequences now ftated
" by Mr. Cornwall, was then given for fhutting
" the door againft all hope ＿＿＿＿＿ ration.
" And fo ftrong was the fp＿＿＿＿＿ the
" new taxes, that the feffion ＿＿cluded with the
" following remarkable declaration. After ftating
" the vigorous meafures which had been purfued,
" the fpeech from the throne proceeds.
" You have affured me of your *firm* fupport in
" the *profecution* of them. Nothing, in my opi-
" nion, could be more likely to enable the well-
" difpofed of my fubjects, in that part of the
" world, effectually to difcourage and defeat the
" defigns of the factious and feditious, than the
" hearty concurrence of every part of the legif-
" lature, *in maintaining the execution of the laws in*
" *every part* of my dominions.——After this no
" man dreamt that a repeal under this miniftry
                                        " could

"could take place." From that promiſe of the commons to ſupport his majeſty, and from the king's
opinion concerning a hearty concurrence of every
branch of the legiſlature *in maintaining the execution
of the laws* in every part of his dominions, he
argues, as if this ſpeech of the king, and declaration of the commons were to be precluſive of
all changes in the laws then ſubſiſting; and thence
he concludes that no repeal would be made under
the preſent miniſtry. And who but ſuch a dreamer
has ever dreamt, that any law has been repealed,
that then exiſted? ſome of the duties, for reaſons
already juſtified, were taken away by a ſubſequent
act. But is the former repealed? is a houſe, that
uſed to be inhabited by ſix people, without an in-
habitant becauſe one alone remains in it? But if
that act be repealed, for what is this dreamer eternally contending?

It is his peculiar excellence to defeat, by a ſubſequent paſſage, what he has advanced in a former. " Five ~~~~ after this ſpeech, the public
" ~~~~ part of which he is going to
" read, was ~~~ by Lord Hiſborough, ſecre-
" tary of ſtate for the colonies. After reciting
" the ſubſtance of the king's ſpeech, he goes on
" thus:

" I can take upon me to aſſure you, notwith-
" ſtanding inſinuations to the contrary, from men
" *with factious and ſeditious views*, that his ma-
" jeſty's *preſent adminiſtration, have at no time*
" *entertained a deſign to propoſe to parliament, to*
" *lay any further taxes upon America, for the pur-*
" *poſe of raiſing a revenue*; and that it is, at pre-
" ſent their intention to propoſe, the next ſeſſion
" of parliament, to take off the duties upon glaſs,
" paper, and colours; upon conſideration of ſuch

" duties

" duties *having been laid contrary to the true prin-*
" *ciples of commerce.*"

" Thefe have always been, and *ftill are,* the
" fentiments of his majefty's *prefent fervants*; and
" by which their conduct, in *refpect to America, has*
" *been governed*; and *his majefty* relies upon your
" prudence and fidelity, for fuch an explanation of
" *his* meafures, as may tend to remove the pre-
" judices which have been excited by the mifre-
" prefentations of thofe who are enemies to the
" peace and profperity of Great Britain and her
" colonies, and to re-eftablifh, that mutual *con-*
" *fidence and affection,* upon which the glory of
" the empire depends."——"Here is a canonical
" book of minifterial fcripture, the general epiftle to
" the Americans;" and you fhall foon be convinced,
that, like a true heterodox commentator, he makes
it fpeak what it does not imply.

He firft afks, " what does Mr. Cornwall fay to
" it ?" What that gentleman faid I know not;
but of this I am certain, that he could have refuted the many confident affertions which this orator
pronounces in immediate fucceffion. Thefe
I will prefume to anfwer. " Here a repeal is
promifed, promifed *without condition,* and while
their authority was actually refifted." The letter of Lord Hillfborough fays, " it is at *prefent*
the intention of adminiftration to *propofe,* the
next feffion of parliament, to take off the duties
upon glafs, paper, and colours; upon confideration of fuch duties having been laid contrary to
the true principles of commerce."

Do thefe words *promife* a repeal of an act, which
only exprefs the *then* intention of the miniftry, to
propofe to parliament the taking away the duties
on glafs, paper, and colours? Can that be a *re-*
peal

peal of an act which leaves it in full energy, respecting the tax on tea ? Can it be a repeal *without*
condition ; when the *condition* is, that the tax on
tea shall continue ? Where then is this promise, without *condition* ? " *I pass by* the pub-
" lic promise of a peer, relative to the repeal of
" taxes by this house. I pass by," says he, " the
" use of the king's name in a matter of supply,
" that sacred and reserved right of the commons."
Is his majesty's name applied in a matter of supply, when it is expressly said, " his majesty relies
" on the prudence and fidelity of the American
" governors, for such an explanation of measures
" as may tend to remove the prejudices which
" have been excited by the misrepresentation of
" those who are enemies to their country." Where
then is this *promise* of a *peer*, relative to the repeal
of taxes ? Where is the *king's name* used in a matter of *supply* ? But things impossible to other men,
by him are easily effected. He can *hear* things
that *no* longer *found* ; and, therefore, he can as
readily *pass by* what *never* did exist. But truth
will sting, though not reclaim, an evil conscience.
He felt for those to whom these misrepresentations
of the *enemies* of Great-Britain and her colonies
were directed. *Vengeance* beholds the straight line
of *verity*, through a medium like an ill made pane
of glass, by which it is distorted from its true di-
rection into a variety of deviations." " I conceal,"
says he, " the ridiculous figure of parliament,
" hurling its thunders at the gigantic rebellion of
" America ; and then, five days after, prostrate at
" the feet of those assemblies they affected to de-
" spise, begging them, by the intervention of
" their ministerial sureties, to receive submission,
" and heartily promising amendment." But where

are

are all thefe difgraceful deeds of parliament to be found ? By what means can a letter from Lord Hillfborough proftrate the parliament at the feet of the American affemblies ? was he ordered by parliament to write that letter ? Wherein confifts the ridiculous figure which parliament hath made by hurling thunders at the gigantic rebellion of America, are they not continued and encreafed ? But in what part of this letter are to be feen this proftration, this begging the affemblies to receive fubmiffion, and this hearty promife of amendment, in oppofition to the infinuations of factious feditious men ? It is indeed faid, the *prefent* adminiftration have not deiigned to propofe any farther taxes on America, for *raifing a revenue* ; is that a fubmiffion ? Is it a proftration to oppofe the malice of men who intend to fubvert their country's rights ? Is it a proftration to take off duties which were contrary to the true principles of commerce ? and that fuch they were, I have fhewn to demonftration. Is it *begging*, to fay his majefty relies on his governors for a refutation of the falfhoods which have been promulged by the enemies both of Britain and her colonies ? Where then is this ridiculous figure to be found, even in the minifter who wrote this letter ? But although no fuch ignominious proceedings be therein to be difcerned, you fhall fpeedily be fhewn by whom this proftration, this begging, this hearty promife of amendment were made, to the indelible difgrace of themfelves ; and by the impious oblation of the rights of Britain to the fhrine of rebellion in America. Is not this opprobrious reprefentation of the Britifh parliament, fomething more than ridiculous in Edmund Burke, Efq ?

" Paffing

" Paffing therefore," fays he, " from the con-
" ftitutional confideration to the mere policy, does
" not this letter imply, that the *idea* of taxing
" America, for the purpofe of a revenue, is an
" abominable project ; when the miniftry fuppofe
" none but factious men, and with feditious views,
" could charge them with it ?" Is it a confequence
that this letter muft imply, that the idea of taxing
America, is an abominable project, becaufe the
miniftry fuppofe that none but *factious* men would
charge them with it ? If none but *virtuous men*, and
good fubjects, had thus accufed them, it might have
been fuppofed to be an *abominable project*. But the
charges of *faction*, which are founded on the principles of *malevolence*, for interefted ends, were
never deemed, till now, to indicate, that the objects which were reprobated, were therefore abominable. This orator enquires into the weight of
all things, as a tanner does into that of an ox's
hide, by dragging it backwards by the tail.

.He continues, " does not this letter adopt and.
" fanctify the American diftinction, of *taxing for*
" *a revenue*." And what if it does, wherein confifts the criminality ? " Does it not formally reject
" all *future* taxation on that principle ?" No ! the
letter exprefsly declares, that his majefty's *prefent
administration*, do not intend to propofe to parliament the laying of any *further* tax for a revenue.
And that it is their *prefent intention* to propofe the
next feffion to take off the duties on glafs, &c.
leaving that on tea.

Do *prefent* intentions *formally reject* all *future*
defigns of taxation for a revenue ? But he con-
founds all *times* and all ideas *prefent* and *future* ;
parts and the *whole*, have no diftinctions in his conception. " Does it not," he adds, " ftate the

F 4   " minifterial

" minifterial rejection of fuch principle of taxa-
" tion, not as the occafional, but the conftant,
" opinion of the king's fervants." It ftates no *rejection* at all. It ftates only, that it was *then* the
intention of the miniftry to lay no *further* taxes
upon the Americans ; and that it was their *then*
intention, to propofe taking off the duties on glafs,
&c. Where is the *principle* of taxation rejected ;
when the tax on tea is continued ? how do thefe
words fignify a *conftant* opinion, and not an *occafional*,
which exprefs it to be the opinion of *that time*, and
on *that occafion*.

He perfifts, " does it not fay (I care not how
" confiftently,) but does it not fay, that their con-
" duct, with regard to America, *has been always*
" governed by this policy ?" That this fpeaker
has no *care* for confiftency, has been evinced beyond difpute. Otherwife, how could he have
afked this queftion ? for what is there that can
prove, that the conduct of the *prefent* miniftry,
has not been governed by that policy ? Were not
thefe duties impofed by the *preceding* miniftry? have
not five of them been repealed by the *prefent* ; does
not this prove, to demonftration, that this conduct
of not taxing for a revenue, is that which has governed the policy of the prefent minifters ?

" It goes further. Thefe excellent and trufty
" fervants of the king, juftly fearful left they
" themfelves fhould have loft all credit with the
" world, bring out the image of their gracious
" fovereign from the inmoft and moft facred fhrine,
" and they pawn him, as a fecurity for their pro-
" mife. *His majefty relies on the prudence and
" fidelity of the commons*," whereas it *was on that of
the governors, for fuch an explanation of his
meafures.

Thus,

Thus, with as much good manners as truth, he represents the miniſtry as a ſet of Popiſh prieſts, who having brought forth his majeſty, as an image in a proceſſion from the inmoſt ſhrine, turn thieves and pledge it to the commons as a ſet of pawn-brokers. But not a ſyllable of all this confident aſſertion is to be found in the letter It has been already proved, that it contains nothing of all that he has aſſerted. Can his majeſty be pledged for that which is *not* in the letter? the king relies on the governours of the provinces to explain his meaſures, to obviate the miſrepreſentations of his and the nation's enemies. Is he thereby pledged as a ſecurity for promiſes? promiſes which you are convinced have no exiſtence? If the world does entertain the leaſt regard for juſtice and for truth, the miniſters will preſerve their credit, and this orator become the univerſal contempt and outcaſt of every true Briton.

The conduct of lord Bottetourt in Virginia, being conſentaneous with lord Hillſborough's letter, that which juſtifies the latter exculpates his lordſhip. I ſhall therefore only obſerve that this orator, ſo over ſcrupulouſly delicate, at the end of what he tranſcribes from lord Bottetourt's ſpeech to the Virginians, has marked the ſubſequent words, by printing them in a different letter from the reſt. "*That his majeſty would rather* " *part with his crown, than preſerve it by deceit.*" The paſſage immediately ſucceeding will probably explain the reaſon of this diſtinction.

" A glorious and true character, which (ſince " the commons ſuffer his miniſters with impunity " to anſwer for his ideas of taxation) they ought " to make it their buſineſs to enable his majeſty " to preſerve it in all its luſtre. Let him have " character,

" character, fince ours is no more. Let fome part
" of the government be kept in refpect."

As no man that does, or ever did exift, has a
more juft claim, from invariable practice, to draw
conclufions, which his premifes will *not* fupport,
I will generoufly allow it him in this inftance.
The plain meaning of the preceding words is this.
Since his majefty's *ideas* of taxation are fuch as the
minifters ought to be *punifhed* for carrying into
execution : and fince the parliament cannot punifh
thefe *iniquitous fervants*, they ought to enable their
mafter, the *contriver* of this *criminal* taxation, to
preferve his *character* in all its luftre. If the orator
chufes to accept this explanation of the preceding
paffage, he ftands only as the moft abfurd of all
reafoners. But I imagine from the diftinctive
manner in which thefe words are printed, " *he*
" *would rather part with his crown, than preferve it*
" *by deceit*," that the preceding paffage was ironically intended. And this I furmife, as much
from the difpofition to malevolence which appears
in this fpeech, as from the difference in the printing. For fuch is the irony of this fpeaker, it con-
veys no hint either of wit or humour, and always
requires italics as an indication of his intention,
the circumftance of malevolence excepted. If it
be irony, he then efcapes the imputation of abfurdity in falfe reafoning in this inftance, and only
charges his fovereign with the character of *deceit-*
ful, which is to be preferved in all its *luftre*. He will
never decide this matter ; to you I leave whether
it is to be imputed to his *head* or to his *heart*.

Such are the comments of this curious commentator ; and now their merit and intent are truly
expofed, I will not injure your good fenfe. I will
not even fuggeft that Britons can remain without
conviction of his heterodoxy, and that the ge-
ge neral

neral epiftle to the Americans is a *canonical* book
of minifterial fcripture. "*What does the gentle-*
"*man fay to that ?*"

He then tells you it was the letter of lord North
and of all the king's then minifters. If they
have as much reafon to be afham.d of that letter,
as he has of his comments, they muft each of
them be endued with more impudence than falls
to the fhare of one man in a million, fhould either
of them dare to fpeak again in parliament.
He then tells you, that "the very firft news that
" a Britifh parliament heard what it was to do
" with the duties which it had granted to the king,
" was by the publication of the votes of Ame-
" rican affemblies. It was in America that your
" refolutions were pre-declared. It was from
" thence that we knew to a certainty how much
" exactly, and not a fcruple more or lefs, we were
" to repeal. We were unworthy to be let into the
" fecret of our own conduct."

The letter fays it was the prefent intention of
the miniftry to propofe, in the *next* feffion of parliament, to take off the duties upon glafs, &c.
As the parliament was prorogued before the
writing of the preceding letter to the American
governours, what reafon was there that the parliament fhould be acquainted before the proro-
gation, with what was intended to be propofed to
them in the next feffion ? and that a fet of men
can be let into the *fecret* of their *own* conduct,
feems to be a conception as abfurd as that of the
perfon who hung a glafs at his bed's foot to fee
how he *looked* when he was *faft afleep.*

" Do you after this, fays he, wonder that you
" have no weight and no refpect in the colonies.
" After this are you furprifed that parliament is
                                              " every

" every day and every where losing (I feel it with
" sorrow, I utter it with reluctance) that reveren-
" tial affection which so endearing a name of au-
" thority ought to carry with it; that you are
" obeyed solely with respect to the bayonet;
" and that this house, the ground and pillar of
" freedom, is itself held up by the treacherous
" underpinning and clumsy buttereffes- of arbi-
" trary power."

Is it not somewhat fingular that an orator, who
is fuppofed equally to underftand every thing to
which he prefumes, fhould reprehend the conduct
of minifters for not preparing the members, when
the parliament was not fitting, for what they were
to do when they did affemble? and that this parliament fhould lofe their reverential affection, becaufe they were *not* treated contrary to the dictates
of this conftitution, by which they are enjoined to
enter the houfe unpreposfessed and unprejudiced?
if the houfe hath loft its endearing name of authority, to whom is it to be afcribed but to this fpeaker
and his affociates, who have filled the minds of the
populace and the Americans with fuch refolutions to
rebellion, as nothing but the bayonet can fubdue?
oh! but the metaphor! the beauty and prefervation of the metaphor! The *houfe* is the *ground* on
which it ftands, it is the *pillar* that ftands on *that*
again, and is *itfelf* held up only by the treacherous
underpinning clumfy *buttereffes* of *arbitrary power*.
And thus this houfe of *freedom* is held up, in this
kingdom, by *that* which has conftantly *overfet* it in
all the other nations of the earth, by the buttereffes
of *treachery* and *arbitrary power*.* Happy Britons,

* Bathos. chap. 5. Of the true genius for the profund, and
by what it is conftituted. He is to mingle bits of the moft
various

tons, you have nought to fear? for, according to the ideas and the words of this profound orator, your liberty can never fail! even arbitrary power props your freedom. If I could suppose him ignorant in *any thing*, from this passage I should think it must be in architecture, from whence he has taken the preceding images. The imaginations of other men have frequently transgressed the laws of nature, and combined the parts of animals that never did exist together. They have made griffins, flying-horses, centaurs, and mermaids. These the pencil may delineate, and fancy conceive the possibility of their existence. But this gentleman's genius despises such tame invention. He overleaps the bounds of *possibility*; combines such things as never can exist together; and resolutely dives into the *profund* beyond those depths to which the most daring mortal hath ever penetrated. Many of our orators have done gloriously, but Burke hath excelled them all!

He advances with equal judgement and rapidity. "If this dignity, which is to stand in the " place of just policy and common sense, had " been consulted, there was a time for preserving " it, and for reconciling it with any concession." Of what can that *dignity* consist, which is to stand in the place of *just policy* and *common sense?* should the preservation of such a *dignity* be ever consulted? can the time have ever arrived for reconciling it with any *concession* but that of *folly?* it is the *peculiar* idea of this gentleman, respecting *dignity*, that

various or discordant kind, as it shall best please his imagination, and contribute to his principal end, which is to glare by strong opposition of colours, *and surprise by contrariety of images.*

that it can be reconcileable with *bad* policy and
folly.

But he is so benignant, he will tell you *how* and
when this wonderful reconciliation might have been
accomplished, " *if* in the session of 1768, that
" session of idle terror and empty menaces, the
" house had, as they were often pressed to do, re-
" pealed the taxes ; then their strong operations
" would have come justified and enforced, in
" case their concessions had been returned by out-
" rages." He has told you the preamble was a
phantom, a quiddity, a thing without substance
or even a name ; therefore, a *nothing*. Is *that*
to be repealed ? He has told you *also* the act *was*
repealed. And now he says, *if* the parliament *had*
repealed this act, and that concession had been returned with outrage, why then their strong
operations would have come justified and enforced.
If this would have preserved the *dignity* of parliament, it must indeed have stood in the place of
just policy and common-sense. But how could it
have reconciled this *dignity* with this *concession* ?
Can the dignity of a state be preserved by sur-
rendering its authority ? and really the imagination, that the Americans would have returned outrages for the concession of what they required ; a
concession that would in fact have given up the
parliamentary right of taxing them, is not a little
extraordinary. If they did not, what cause could
the parliament have had for enforcing ? Does it
not seem, as if he were convinced that these repub-
lican fanatics would *not* have accepted of any advantage that is *not* obtained by *rebellion ?* and
therefore, that such strong operations would have
been necessary ?

" The

" The commons," as he declares, " began with
" violence; and before terrors could have any
" effect, good or bad, the minifters immediately
" begged pardon, and promifed that repeal to.
" the Americans, which they had refufed to an
" eafy, good-natured, complying Britifh parlia-
" ment." As to the begging pardon, and promifed repeal, thofe circumftances are difpatched.
But how will this orator reconcile that the fame
parliament, which pronounced terror and menaces
to the Americans, becaufe they would not comply
with the taxes, fhould be an eafy, good-natured,
complying parliament that requefted this repeal?
or if they inclined to the repeal; what could have
prevented them from paffing it?

> Diforder in variety we fee,
> And here, as all things differ, none agree.

" The affemblies which had been publicly and
" avowedly diffolved, for *their* contumacy, are
" called together to receive the parliament's fub-
" miffion." Enough has been faid on that fubmiffion. " The minifterial directors bluftered like
" magic tyrants here; and then went mumping
" with a fore leg in America, canting, and
" whining, and complaining of faction, which re-
" prefented them as friends to a revenue from the
colonies." Had *all* the minifterially directing
mumpers, but *one* fore leg among them? Did they
take *it* by *turns* through the provinces, or how
did they manage it? but I will foon fhew who
were in reality the minifterially directing *mumpers*,
and reftore the *fore leg* to that *body* to which it
alone belongs.

" i hope," fays he, " no body in this houfe
" will hereafter have the *impudence* to defend
                                   " American

" American taxes in the name of miniftry." I alfo fhould have *my* hope, if any good were to be expected from this orator, that he would never more have the *impudence* to calumniate the miniftry on the fubject of American taxes. " The " moment they do," fays he, " with this letter of " attorney in his hand, he will tell them, in the " authorifed terms, they are wretches *with factious* " *and feditious views ; enemies to the peace and pro-* " *fperity of the mother country and the colonies,* and " fubverters *of the mentual affection and confidence* " *on which the glory and fafety of the Britifh empire* " *depend.*" Will thofe words, derived from the conduct of him and his confederates, authorife him to pronounce them againft thofe who fhall defend the miniftry in tranfactions fo juft and defenfible ? No ! he will not attempt it. He will never more produce that paper which is now fo fully proved to falfify his affertions. Even he, this orator, will be too fcrupuloufly delicate to produce, a fecond time, a plenary refutation of all he has compelled that paper to imply.

" After this letter," he adds, " the queftion is " no more on propriety or dignity ; they are gone " already. The faith of your fovereign is pledged " to the political principle. The general declara-" tion in the letter goes to the whole of it." The falfity of all this hath been already evinced ; it will be endlefs to anfwer a tedious repetition of the fame miftakes. But mind the dictatorial fpirit of this Edmund Burke, Efq; once private fecretary to Lord Rockingham, to the commons of this realm, " you muft," fays he, " therefore either " abandon the fcheme of taxing, or you muft fend " the minifters tarred and feathered to America, " who dared to hold out the royal faith for a re-
" nunciation

" nunciation of all taxes for revenue. Them you
" muſt puniſh, or this faith you muſt preſerve."
That no ſuch faith, for a renunciation of ſuch taxes,
was ever held out, has been already proved to
demonſtration. Appeal to the letter of Lord
Hillſborough. Again be ſatisfied. There was a
time when the commons of Britain would not have
borne ſo dictatorial an inſult, founded on the miſ-
repreſentation and calumny of their own transacti-
ons. In thoſe days, had he uttered ſuch atrocious
terms, he would himſelf have been metaphorically
tarred, and *papered* with his ſpeech; and ſent where-
ever he pleaſed to go, except into that houſe.
But another puniſhment awaits him. His *oration*
commits ſelf-murder. On this inqueſt it will be
buried in a croſs-way, and a ſtake driven through
it, as a warning to all future ſpeakers, not to rely
on *ſound* without *ſenſe*.

" This preſervation of the royal faith," he adds,
" is of more conſequence than the duties on *red*
" *lead* or *white lead*, or on broken *glaſs*, or *atlas*,
" ordinary, or *demi fine*, or *blue royal*, or *baſtard*,
" or *fool's-cap*, which they have given up, or the
" three-pence on tea, which they retained." And
I will add, of more conſequence than all the *fools*,
who pretending to be ſpeakers, are eternally
evincing their want of intellect. But reflect, I intreat you, with what propriety this opinion, of the
preſervation of the royal faith, iſſues from the lips
of him, who, with his maſter, gave up the royal
faith which had been pledged, in the miniſtry of
Mr. Grenville, to ſupport the parliament in their
reſolves to ſuſtain his majeſty againſt the revolt
of the Americans. This how ſhamefully they
gave up, ſhall be proved when I come to examine
the Rockingham adminiſtration.

From

From what motives do thefe eternal and felf-contradictory affertions fpring? Is it from inability to comprehend the plain expreffions of Lord Hillfborough's letter? is it from an incapacity to draw juft conclufions from his own promifes? Does he imagine, that he can hold the underftandings of mankind within a circle that they cannot pafs, as conjurors are faid to treat the devil? Is it from revenge, from defperation, from *invidioufnefs*? Aye, *that is the caufe that makes this fpeech of fo long breath.* " The miniftry which is here fhining in " riches, in favour, and in power, and urging the " punifhment of that very offence to which this " orator and his affociates had been the temp-" ters."

He continues, " If reafons, refpecting fimply " your own commerce, which is your own con-", venience, were the fole grounds of the repealing " of the five duties, why does Lord Hillfborough, " in difclaiming in the name of the king and mi-" nifters, their ever having had an intent to tax " for revenue, mention it as the means of re-efta-" blifhing the confidence and affection of the co-" lonies?" But wherein hath his lordfhip *difclaimed*, in the name of the king and minifters, their *ever* having had an intent to tax for revenue? his letter exprefsly declares the contrary; that the prefent adminiftration have no defign to lay any *farther* taxes upon America for a revenue. The term *farther* abfolutely implies, as the fact does verify, that they were *already* laid for that end. How then will he explain, that what has *never been faid* can have been *mentioned*, as the means of re-eftablifhing the confidence of the colonies? I will prefume once to anfwer for him. By confounding, in his ufual manner, times paft with times to come,

and

and things that never did exist with assertions that
they have existed.

"Is it a way of soothing *others*, says he, "to
"assure them that you will take good care of
"yourself?" It is indeed a very mistaken way.
But where does he find it? Not in Lord Hillsborough's letter; for therein it is said, that his lordship "will be content to be declared infamous, if
"he does not, to the last hour of his life, exert
"every power, in order to obtain and maintain,
"for the continent of America, that satisfaction
"which he has been authorised to promise." Has
it been violated? Do these expressions assure the
Americans, that *he* will take good *care* of *himself*,
which promise that *care* of *them?*

"The medium, the only medium, for regain-
"ing the American affection and confidence, is,
"that you will take off something oppressive to
"their minds." Have you ever heard till now of
a medium *for* regaining affection? is the *will*
of taking something from their minds a *medium?*
However, to understand what his words do not
express, and yet as he meant them, let me ask
you if he be not a man to whom experience has
not taught wisdom? or could he, who advised,
harangued and voted, for the repeal of the stamp
act, have said, that the removal of oppression will
regain confidence in America? If what is oppressive to the minds of men be a reason for re-
moving it, what law can then remain unabrogated? Will not the murderer, the felon, the
cheat, the impostor, and every species of villains,
revolt against the parliamentary authority until the
statutes, which oppress their minds, be taken off?
The blind see nothing. They know their condition, and feel their way with a stick. If this orator

would

would follow their example, he would not so constantly *run against* the *facts* which *stand* in his
way.

He says, " the letter strongly enforces the idea,
" of easing their minds by taking away *all* taxes,"
and yet that letter does absolutely leave the tea tax
unrepealed.

He persists, " for though the repeal of the taxes
" be promised on commercial principles, yet the
" means of counteracting *the insinuations of men with*
" *seditious and factious views*, is by a disclaimer of
" the intention of taxing for revenue, as a con-
" stant invariable sentiment, and rule of conduct
" in the government of America." There is
something, to my comprehension, not a little ænig-
matical in this passage. The *repeal* of the taxes is
promised on commercial principles : yet the *means*
of counteracting the insinuations of men with factious and seditious views, is by a disclaimer of the
intention of taxing for revenue, as a constant invariable sentiment, and rule of conduct in the government of America. But there exists no disclaimer, as it has been already proved; and thus the
means consist in that which has *no* existence.

" I remember," says he, " Lord North, *not in*
" *a former debate, to be fair*, (it would be disor-
" derly to refer to it, I suppose I read it some-
" where,) but the noble lord was pleased to say,
" that he did not conceive how it could enter into
" the head of man, to impose those taxes which
" he voted for imposing, and voted for repeal-
" ing ; as being taxes contrary to all the princi-
" ples of commerce, laid on *British manufactures*."
Oh! what a namby pamby attempt to wit or humour do, *his to be sure, and his suppose he read it*
somewhere, exhibit.

This

This he adduces as an instance of his lordship's inconsistency and self-contradiction. But I will prove that it is consistent in every part, and consentaneous with the strictest integrity. When these taxes were laid, his lordship was not a minister. He knew *then* what he since expressed as above. His motive for voting them was the reinstating of the parliamentary authority. The taxes were estimated as a secondary consideration. He knew that every day's delay encreased the danger of annihilating the former, and therefore that it was not to be postponed. He knew the latter might be repealed on some subsequent occasion. Such were then his views. Since the time he has been minister, he has verified his opinion, by an actual repeal of those taxes on British manufactures ; and he has preserved the duty on tea for the sake of sustaining the sovereign authority, which was his original and sole motive. Hence it appears, that voting at first for the imposition, and subsequently for the repeal, are neither inconsistency nor contradiction in his lordship's conduct. Painters, who wish to draw justly, practise the custom of placing their portraits before a glass, and examining them in the reflected image. By these means, a number of errors are remarked and corrected, which had otherwise escaped. It would be well judged in this orator, if he would imitate that custom ; and consider his speeches in the reflexion of a better judgement than his own, before he printed them *at least*. It is true indeed the sufferings of vanity might be so grievous, by these means, that probably an orator for rebellion would be lost. But the commons would receive the vast advantage of being freed from so much senseless sound and self-contradiction.

G 3

" He

He grows audacious. " He *dares* fay the noble
" lord is perfectly well read, becaufe the duty of
" his particular office requires he fhould be fo, in
" all our revenue laws, and in the policy which is
" to be collected out of them." From the peculiar kind of politenefs which he has fhewn this
nobleman, throughout his fpeech, I fuggeft this
to be intended for irony. I could wifh in fuch inftances of attempting to be *humourous* or *witty*, he
would follow the example of a fign painter, who
could draw but one thing, which was the white rofe.
In confequence of his *genius* being tethered to that
alone, he kept a number of figns ready painted,
and then wrote under the white rofe, by way of
note, this is the fign of the *black* dog, or the *red
lion*; as his chapman chofe his fign fhould be. A
note for the future, *this is irony*, this is *wit*, or this
is *humour*, under the paffages which he intends to
pafs for fuch, would be a very convenient indication to his readers. But let me ferioufly afk
this confident fpeaker, whether it be not the *duty*
of *one*, who arraigns the conduct of *others*, to be
perfectly well read in the fubject on which he
fpeaks? hath he obferved that rule in this fpeech?

" Now, fays he, when his lordfhip had read
" this act of American revenue, and a little re-
" covered from his aftonifhment, I fuppofe he
" made *one* ftep *retrograde* (it is but *one*) and look-
" ed at the act which ftands juft *before* it in the
" ftatute book." What could be the caufe of his
lordfhip's aftonifhment at reading an act with
which he had been well acquainted, during its
paffing through the houfe, feems difficult to be
conceived by a common underftanding. But
is there not fomething as truly aftonifhing in this
orator's penetration. He has difcovered that *one*
ftep

ſtep *retrograde* is but *one*; and that his lordſhip
made this ſtep *backwards*, to look at ſomething
that ſtood *before* his laſt object. He then tells you
" of the duties laid on the commodities imported
" into the iſle of Man, that the two acts perfectly
" agree in all reſpects except one, which is, that
" the duties are a great deal higher on the things
" imported into the iſle, than into the continent
" of America. And that both acts were exactly
" the ſame for raiſing revenues. He then aſks,
" will the noble lord condeſcend to tell him why
" he repealed the taxes on your manufactures ſent
" out to America, and not the taxes on the ma-
" nufactures exported to the iſle of Man? the
" principle was exactly the ſame, the objects
" charged infinitely more extenſive, the duties
" without compariſon higher. Why." He *aſks*
his lordſhip, and anſwers *himſelf*. " Why not-
" withſtanding all his childiſh pretexts, becauſe
" the taxes were quickly ſubmitted to in the iſle
" of Man, and becauſe they raiſed a flame in
" America, their reaſons were political not com-
" mercial."

I have already repeatedly ſhewn you that the
principle of the American act was to re-eſtabliſh the
ſupreme legiſlature of this realm; and that the taxes
were the means of doing it. The act relative to the
iſle of Man had no ſuch motive, it was ſolely for
raiſing a revenue. Your orator, however, who is
conſtantly engaged in ſetting things up for the ſake
of overthrowing them himſelf, as *children* build
houſes with cards, is on this occaſion, as is cuſ-
tomary, kind enough to refute what his queſtion
propoſes. " It was becauſe the taxes were *quietly*
" ſubmitted to in the iſle of Man, and becauſe
" they raiſed a *flame* in America." Did he expect

the

the noble lord would repeal thofe taxes which the Manckfmen quietly received? and when the flame which was raifed, had heated the Americans to a degree of not receiving the Britifh manufactures, whilft the duties were on them, did there not arife a juft caufe for repealing thofe duties, that the manufacturers might not be lefs employed in England? and thus thofe two things which are *exactly the fame* are *totally diffimilar.* I prefume the reafons of lord North for repealing five of the American taxes were both *political* and *commercial.* That they were commercial I have fufficiently fhewn, and by what magic this fpeaker can divide *commerce* from *policy* in this inftance, *he* muft explain; or *you* yourfelves difcover; it exceeds my comprehenfion.

He then returns, like a mifer's ghoft to his hidden treafure, and afferts " the repeal was made as " lord Hillfborough's letter well expreffes it, to " acquire *the confidence and affection of the colonies,* " *on which the glory and fafety of the Britifh empire* " *depends.*" The letter exprefsly pronounces that the taxes were repealed on *the true principles of commerce;* and that the glory and fafety of the Britifh empire depended on effacing the mifreprefentations of the *enemies* of her empire. Even this orator, in the preceding page, declares that the letter fays, " *the repeal of the taxes was promifed on commercial* " *principles.*" Will he neither believe himfelf nor the letter? how then can he expect that the world will give credit to what he avers?

However, let it be imagined that the duties have been repealed for the reafons which he afcribes to lord Hillfborough. " That, he fays, was " a wife and juft motive furely, if ever there was " fuch. But the mifchief and the difhonour is,
" that

" that they have not done what they had given
" the colonies juft caufe to expect, when the mi-
" nifters difclaimed the taxing for a revenue."
Hence it appears that the repeal, which he fays
was *made* on a wife and juft motive, was not *made*
at all ; becaufe the mifchief and difhonour *is,*
that the minifters ha e *not* done what they had
given the colonies juft reafon to expect, when they
difclaimed the idea of taxing for a revenue. And
thus this mifchief, this difhonour arofe from *not*
having *done* that which they had *done* by the repeal;
or from difregarding the *promife* of a *difclaimer*
which, it has been incontrovertibly proved, they
never did *promife.*

In fact, this orator's potatoe bed of fallacy,
abfurdity, and felf-contradiction, is fo extremely
prolific : they fhoot from one another in fuch
amazing numbers, that no labour, no induftry,
no art, can clear the ground of their fuper-
abundance.

And now for a rant of *exclamation* moft over
fcrupuloufly delicate, " there is nothing fimple,
" nothing manly, nothing ingenuous, open, de-
" cifive, or fteady, in the proceeding with regard
" either to the continuance or repeal of the taxes.
" The whole has an air of littlenefs and fraud."
It is a painful tafk fo conftantly to return to the
refuting of what has been already fo repeatedly
difproved. Yet fuch is the confidence of this
fpeaker and his affociates, that if a fingle circumftance, although it be exactly fimilar to what has
been already refuted, be left unanfwered, they
will unanimoufly pronounce, it is unanfwerable. I
therefore intreat your patience in the prolixity of
this reply. And although I may with fafety refer
you to the narrative already given of minifterial
conduct

conduct in this affair, yet to preclude every means of his eluding a defeat, I will examine this explosion of verbosity.

The simpleness of every undertaking consists in its being compounded of as few objects as possible. In this instance, it consists of two alone; those of restoring the supreme authority to exertion and vigour in America, and of imposing a tax as the means of obtaining that end. Thus the *end* and the *means* constitute but *two*. Can he conceive an undertaking in which there are neither means nor object? is he so skilled in any art, that he can so simplify *two* things as to make them less than *two?* where then is the want of its being *simple*. Wherein consists the defect of manliness? the act indeed imposed taxes, on several commodities, in a former administration, which lord North then disliked. They were repealed, since he was minister, for commercial reasons. But the duty on tea does still preserve that act in as much energy as before: and the means which are now employing evince that it is supported by manliness. But that Edmund Burke, who advised, harangued, and voted for the pusillanimous retreat of his master before rebellion, without risking an engagement, should charge the ministry with unmanliness, is an act of confidence not easily to be equalled. And as nonsense can never be more justly applied than to him, it may be said, *none but himself can be his parallel.*

Return to lord Hillsborough's letter, you will there be convinced that nothing can be more ingenuous, open, decisive, or steady, in the proceeding, with regard either to the continuance or the repeal of the taxes. You are therein told that the five duties are only intended to be repealed; that it was the present intention of the minister

to lay no more taxes for a revenue; that his lordship pledged his honour for the truth of these
things. All thele particulars have been moſt re-
ligiouſly obſerved. From whence then does this
charge ariſe, of diſingenuous concealment, inde-
ciſion, verſatility, with regard either to the continuance or repeal of the taxes? from the dictates
of a *heart*, which wants nothing but the ability
of a *head* to ſpread deſtruction on the conſtitution
of this country. What a felicity it is, that the
powers of men are inadequate to their wills on
ſuch occaſions! but the moſt extravagant inſtance
of this rant is, his branding the miniſtry, and even
the parliament with having acted with *littleneſs* and
fraud. And this ignominy, which, it ſeems, the
liberty of ſpeech allows to be *pronounced* in parliament, he has *publiſhed* to the world. It is an
act as becoming *him* to *do*, as for *them* to *ſuffer*.

He perſeveres, " the article of tea is ſlurred
" over in the circular letter as it were by acci-
" dent.—Nothing is ſaid of a reſolution either
" to keep that tax, or to give it up. There is
" no fair dealing in any part of the tranſaction."
In what does it appear that the article of tea was
ſlurred over as by accident? is not the poſitive
mention of the other five taxes being to be repealed, without ſpeaking of that on tea, as expreſſive,
and as clear, that it was to be continued, as if it had
been attended with a thouſand aſſeverations? Was
it not in that ſenſe underſtood by the Americans?
becauſe he has told you that *one* ſtep is but *one*,
does he imagine it neceſſary to declare a reſolution,
that what is ſeen to be abſolutely *reſerved*, is *not* to
be *given away*? if returning from a journey, he
orders his ſervant to take off his boots, does
he think it neceſſary to tell him he muſt
leave

leave on his ftockings? I will now afk him where
is *his fair dealing in any part of this tranfaction.*

Like a fox that conftantly returns to the fame
cover from which he has been frequently hunted,
that by leading the hounds through brakes and
briars, and by earthing at laft, hath eluded the
purfuit of the huntfmen ; fo this orator returning
to the fame fubject, expects by leading you
through the brambles of abfurdity and felf-contradiction, and by diving into the vaft profund, eternally to efcape. The fubfequent paffage
is an inftance of his defign. " If you mean,"
fays he, " to follow your true motives and your
" public faith, give up your tax on tea for raifing
" a revenue, the principle of which has, in effect,
" been difclaimed in your name, and which pro-
" duces you no advantage ; no, not a penny. Or
" if you choofe to go on with a poor pretence,
" inftead of a folid reafon, and will ftill adhere to
" your *cant* of commerce; you have ten thoufand
" times more ftrong commercial reafons for giving
" up this duty on tea; than for abandoning the
" five others, that you have already renounced."

This paffage is addreffed to the commons. He
prefumes to bid them follow their *true motives* and
their public *faith*, to give up the tax on tea, the
principle of which has been difclaimed in their
name. This alludes to lord Hillfborough's letter,
in which not a fyllable is faid of the commons,
but that the miniftry intend to *propofe* to parliament to take off the tax. The faith of parliament
has never been either mentioned or alluded to
in that letter; and as to the difclaimer, that falfity
hath been fufficiently exploded. However, in
plain Englifh, it is. If you choofe to go on with
your poor pretence, you are a pack of fellows
without

without folid reafon, and *canters* on commerce. I
fhall leave the commons to anfwer, or to acquiefce
in thefe charges as they pleafe. As to the ten
thoufand times ftronger commercial reafons for
giving up the duty on tea, than the others, I will
give no farther anfwer.

" The American confumption of tea, is an-
" nually, I believe, worth 300,000*l.* at the leaft
" farthing. If you urge the American violence
" as a juftification of your perfeverance in enforc-
" ing this tax, you know that you can never an-
" fwer this plain queftion: Why did you repeal
" the others given in the fame act, whilft the very
" fame violence fubfifted?" But where is this
violence urged as a juftification of perfevering to
enforce this tax? Eftablifh the *if* and you fhall
have the *anfwer*. But without that the truth fhall
be told you. The taxes were not repealed to ap-
peafe the violence, but for commercial reafons. The
tea tax was continued, becaufe that violence fhould
not be complied with, but fubdued. " But," fays
he, " you did not find that violence ceafe upon
" that conceffion." The miniftry did never expect it. They had been long convinced, by his
and his min fters *conceffion*, that their outrage would
be rather encreafed: and therefore they prepared
to defeat that violence by other means than conceffions. But let me give you his anfwer: " No.
" Becaufe the conceffion was far fhort of anfwer-
" ing the principle which Lord Hillfborough had
" abjured, or even the pretence on which the re-
" peal of the other taxes was announced." What
principle is it that his lordfhip hath abjured? Not
the principle of re-eftablifhing the fupreme authority over the Americans, becaufe the tax is left to
fuftain its right. Not that of impofing no further

taxes

taxes on America, becaufe that is alfo preferved. But what is the plain Englifh of *fatisfying a principle?* The pretence, as he calls it, the true commercial principle, on which the repeal of the other taxes was announced, was certainly carried into execution. But will not every conceffion be fhort of fatisfying the Americans, that does not yield a plenary renunciation of the Britifh fovereignty to the demands of rebellion? Is that the fatisfaction which he urges to be granted?

He continues attempting to reafon, "and becaufe,
" by enabling the Eaft-India company to open a
" fhop for defeating the American refolution not to
" pay that fpecific tax, you manifeftly fhewed a
" hankering after the principle of the act, which
" you formerly had renounced."

What fort of fhop it was the Eaft-India company were enabled to open; and how effectually it defeated the American refolution, of not paying the tax; the breaking open the fhips which carried the tea to the colonies, the committing felony, and throwing the tea into the rivers, fufficiently explain. But I conceive thefe fhops can not be properly faid to be for defeating, although they may for eftablifhing the refolution of *not* paying the tax. That this attempt, to enable the company, fhewed fomething more than a hankering after the principle of the act, the fupport of the parliamentary authority, I readily agree. But I abfolutely deny, becaufe it has been irrefragably proved, that this principle was ever renounced.

" Whatever road you take," fays he, " tends
" to a compliance with this motion. It opens to
" you at the end of every vifto. Your commerce,
" your policy, your promifes, your reafons, your
" pretences, your confiftency, your inconfiftency —
" all

" all jointly oblige you to this repeal." Such
being the cafe, that all things, and even thofe
that were never conjoined in the promotion of the
fame event till this hour, *Confiftency* with *inconfiftency*, are united to oblige the miniftry to repeal
this act, why, in the name of nonfenfe, has this
orator beftowed fo much lung-labour in perfuad-
ing them to *accomplifh* that which they are *necef-
fitated* ro perform? As when an alarm is given at
the door of a dove-houfe, the pigeons hurry out
in confufion at the top of it, and leave their nefts
and young to whatever may arrive: fo in any com-
motion from within, the words of this orator prefs
in tumult through his mouth, and leave the half-
hatched and unfledged ideas never to attain ma-
turity.

Every ftep he takes he advances in his confidence of affertion. " It ftill fticks in our throats,
" if we go fo far, the Americans will go farther.
" We do not know that." By this he muft certainly
mean they do *not* know whether it *fticks in their
throats* or not. For it has been *long known*, that
they have already gone *farther* on *conceffion.*
" However," he fays, " the houfe ought from ex-
" perience rather prefume the contrary." I will
appeal to this experience for a refutation of what
he fays. When the duty on molaffes was ordered
to be ftrictly collected, in Mr. Grenville's miniftry,
and other things were enacted, difpleafing to the
Americans, they made no oppofition to the legiflative authority of this realm. They acquiefced
therewith, and petitioned parliament for redrefs.
When the ftamp act was oppofed in parliament, and
that fplit-devil diftinction of the legiflature, into the
right of laying external, and not internal, taxes on
the colonies was engendered, this opinion was
greedily

greedily adopted by the Americans. It was foſ-
tered by the repeal of the ſtamp act. And then the
perſuaſion prevailed among them, that the legiſlature of Britain had no right to tax them, either
externally or internally. In conſequence of this
progreſſion in the principles of rebellion, when the
external duties were laid on goods imported into
America, they openly refuſed to obey the legiſlative authority; advanced to felony; and are now
in actual rebellion. As all theſe were the conſequences of *conceſſion*, ought not the parliament to
conclude, from experience, that a *farther conceſſion* will create ſtill greater demands, until there be
nothing left to be conceded?

   " Can they do more, or can they do worſe, if
" the Commons yield this point?" he aſks. He
anſwers, " he thinks this conceſſion will rather fix
" a turnpike to prevent their farther progreſs."
The queſtion, ſingular as it is, is a mere nothing in compariſon with the anſwer. It is indeed a
ſingular conception, that men who can do nothing
more, n‹ r worſe, ſhould be indulged, with any
thing without correction. But let me come to
the turnpike. The thing which is to ſet up and *fix*
this turnpike, to prevent their farther progreſs, is
the *taking down* of an act of parliament, that will
not let them go through *without* paying. Now, by
what genius, by what art, this cunning-man can
make the taking *down* of a law, that ſtops them
until they pay, and thereby leaving the paſſage abſolutely free, can be *like fixing* a *turnpike* to *prevent*
their farther progreſs, is a *ſimilitude* in which I can
ſee *no* likeneſs. However, it is not without a precedent equally pre-eminent. When May Drum-
mon, in one of *her* holdings forth, to a quaking
congregation, was ſpeaking of the world, ſhe told
                                               them,

them, it was as *round* —— as *round* —— as a horse's
head. Such is the amazing resemblance between
the intellectual faculties of these two celebrated
speakers.

"It is impossible," he says, "to answer for
"bodies of men." Or single ones either, were
they all like this orator. "But he is sure the
"natural effect of fidelity, clemency, kindness in
"governors, is peace, good-will, order, and
"esteem, on the part of the governed." And so
am I too; but not towards rebels. Has he not
been taught the contrary by the repeal of the stamp
act? He seems not to distinguish between the effects of concession to dutiful and to rebellious subjects. The history of Charles the first irrefragably
evinces, that every concession of that king to the
progenitors of these men, who were then rebels,
as their descendants now are, inflamed their impudence; encreased their outrages; and aggrava-
ted their demands; until by consecutive yieldings
to all they asked, that sovereign was murdered;
the people robbed, of their rights of election by
their representatives voting themselves an *eternal*
parliament; and the constitution fundamentally
subverted. Every concession *then*, as in the case
of the Rockingham concession *since*, strengthened
their persuasion that *fear* had been the motive to it;
that the same dastardly spirit would constantly give
way before their most atrocious demands; and that
nothing would be denied. Is it ignorance in the
nature of humankind? Is it a prepense design
to subvert the state, rather than yield to reason?
or is it *self-interest*, which, counteracting all the sa-
lutary proceedings of the ministry, and every virtue of highest estimation among mankind that urges

H   this

this man to involve this nation in ruin, rather than
not to avert his own.

"And now," says he, "Mr. Cornwall having
"spoken what he thought neceffary upon the
"narrow part of the subject, I have given him, I
"hope, a fatisfactory anfwer." If his hope of a
joyful refurrection, be not more *fure* and *certain*,
than this of having fatisfied Mr. Cornwall; or any
man of common-fenfe, he cannot do better than
follow the attorney's example, in a vifion of Don
Quivedo, and prepare himfelf with a fpeech, in
order to plead a demurrer on the day of judgment.

He continues, "Mr. Cornwall next preffes him
"by a variety of *direct* challenges, and *oblique* re-
"flexions, to fay fomething on the hiftorical
"part." This Mr. Cornwall is a dreadful adverfary, he attacks him *alone* in *front* and *flank*.
You fhall fee how he defends himfelf. On this
account "he will open himfelf fully on that im-
"portant and delicate fubject: not for the fake
"of telling Mr. Speaker a long ftory, which he
"knows Mr. Speaker is not particularly fond of,
"but for the fake of the weighty *inftructions*
"that he *flatters* himfelf will neceffarily refult
"from it."

You cannot have forgotten, that in his exordium he *exclaims*, "that for *nine long years*, feffion
after feffion, the Commons had been lafhed
round and round a miferable circle, till their
heads turned giddy, and their ftomachs turned *up*
the arguments they had received." And now he
enters into a continuance of that long nine years
lafhing, in a *long* ftory, for the fake of the weighty
inftructions the houfe may receive. And this he
undertakes, although, he had affured you in
that

that exordium, that " invention was exhaufted ; reafon fatigued ; and experience had given judgement." Is it, therefore, to be admired, that neither Mr. Speaker nor the members are fond of fuch long and fickening ftories?

It feems indeed to be no common act of *felf-adulation*, in Mr. Burke, to imagine, after all the preceding time and circumftances, that *he* alone fhould conceive that his invention was not exhaufted, nor his reafon fatigued. For if he did not fecretly except himfelf, by what means could he have found *inftructions* in this inftance? The plain meaning of all this is, you the Commons of Great Britain, are five hundred and fifty-feven fuch thick-fculled rafcals, that after being lafhed for nine long years, till your inventions were exhaufted, and your reafons fatigued, if you had any, you remain fo egregioufly ignorant of this important fubject, that I, who alone underftand it, am obliged to tell you a long ftory for the fake of *inftructing* you in that which is neceffary for you to know. In what a miferable fituation muft the prefent parliament have been, had not Mr. Burke been re-elected a reprefentative! From whom could they have had one word of weighty inftruction, fince he muft have run away with all the underftanding of the houfe. Thus an *over-fcrupulous delicacy* of affuming fuperior knowledge, like the light in the glowworm's tail, fhines in this orator, and difcovers itfelf the more evidently by means of that impervious obfcurity which furrounds him in the fenate. He is the pillar of fmoke by day, and of fire by night, that guides them through the wildernefs of America.

H 2 However

However, he promiſes, " it ſhall not be longer,
" if he can help it, than ſo ſerious a matter re-
" quires." And then, with a view to keep his
word and *ſhorten* his ſtory, he aſks permiſſion
" to lead the Commons *very far back*, back to the
" act of navigation, the corner ſtone of the po-
" licy of this country, with regard to the co-
" lonies."

" That policy," he continues, " was from the
" beginning purely commercial, and the com-
" mercial ſyſtem was wholly reſtrictive. It was
" the ſyſtem of a monopoly. No trade was let
" looſe from that conſtraint, but merely to enable
" the coloniſts to diſpoſe of what in the courſe of
" your trade you could not take ; or to enable
" them to diſpoſe of ſuch articles as we forced up-
" on them, and for which, without ſome degree
" of liberty, they could not pay.——This prin-
" ciple of commercial monoply, runs through no
" leſs than twenty-nine acts of parliament, from
" the year 1666, to the unfortunate period of
" 1764." The nature and effects of this ſyſtem
of a monopoly ſhall be explained to you in a ſubſequent part of this anſwer.

" In all thoſe acts," he adds, " the ſyſtem of
" commerce is eſtabliſhed as that from whence
" alone you propoſe to make the coloniſts contri-
" bute" (he means directly, and by the operation
of the ſuperintending legiſlative power) " to the
" ſtrength of the empire. He *ventures* to ſay,
" that during that whole period, a parliamentary
" revenue from thence was never *once* in *contem-*
" *plation*." I ſhould indeed have entertained a
leſs doubt, that this accurate ſpeaker does really
know all that was in *contemplation*, during that period and on that ſubject, in the heads of other men,

if

(101)

if he had fhewn himfelf to be better acquainted
with that which hath *paffed* in his *own*. However, he hath wonderful gifts from nature. And as
he *bears* what has done *founding*, why may he not
have perceived all that hath paffed fixty years before he was born? whatever may be your conclufion
on that head, you will not deny him the merit of
being an *adventurer*.

" Accordingly, fays he, in all the number of
" laws paffed, with regard to the plantations, the
" words which diftinguifh revenue laws fpecifically
" as fuch, were, he thinks, premeditately avoid-
" ed." He allows that " a form of words certain-
" ly does not alter the nature of the law, nor
" abridge the power of the law-giver. He ftates
" thefe facts to fhew, not what was the parlia-
" mentary right, but what has been the fettled
" policy. Our revenue laws have *ufually* a *title*
" purporting their being *grants*; and the words *give*
" *and grant*, *ufually* precede the enacting parts."
" From this premife, which expreffes a *cuftom* to
be *ufual*, and therefore does confequently imply that
it was *fometimes obferved*, and at *others not*, he
draws an *abfolute* conclufion, that the terms *give*
and grant being omitted in the acts, relative to
America, render them not laws for a revenue,
an induction which nothing but an *univerfal practice*, of inferting the preceding words into all our
revenue laws, can warrant. For as the *omiffion* of
them is *ufual*, as well as the *infertion*, that omiffion
affords a precedent for their being as legally to be
left out, as the other to be inferted in all fuch ftatutes.
This is the precedent which the parliament obferved
in the revenue acts relative to America. And therefore when " duties were impofed on the colonifts
in acts of king Charles the fecond, and in acts

H 3   of

of William, though no one title of giving *an aid to his majesty*, or any other of the usual titles to revenue acts, was to be found in any of them till 1764." It is evident they were nevertheless *revenue laws*, according to *usual* custom.

He then adds, " nor were the words *give and* " *grant*, in any preamble, until the 6th of George " the second, 1773." And hence it results, that although he *thought* the words *give and grant* were *premeditately left out* of the American acts for 104 years, he *knew* them *premeditately to be put in* for 44 of that time. Hence it is evident also, that these words "which distinguish revenue laws spe- " cifically as such, were no innovation in 1764, because they had been thus applied more than thirty years before that time. The means, by which he attempts to evade the contradiction which that act gives to his preceding assertion, are not less curious than the assertion itself. " However," says he, " the title of this act of George the se- " cond, notwithstanding the words of donation, " considers it merely as a regulation of trade, *an* " *act for the better securing the trade of his majesty's* " *sugar colonies in America*." And thus according to this orator's mode of arguing, the mention of the word *trade*, for which *money* is given by par- liament, makes it no *donation*. And for the same reason, if a man christens his son by the name of *Mary* his *sex* is changed. Would an act, raising money for the better security of the linnen *trade* of his majesty's kingdom of Ireland, followed by the words *give and grant*, be no donation, because it was to regulate trade ?

To the preceding he adds, " the act of George " the second was made on a compromise of all, " and at the express desire of a part of the co-
" lonies

" lonies themſelves. It was therefore, in ſome
" meaſure, with their conſent ; and having a title
" directly purporting only a *commercial regulation*,
" and being in truth nothing more, the words
" were paſſed by, at a time when no jealouſy was
" entertained, and things were little ſcrutini-
" zed." You ſhall ſoon diſcern, how ridiculouſly
he wriggles, to get out of an uneaſy ſituation ;
like a bad horſeman with a galled backſide, and
yet can find no remiſſion of his ſoreneſs.

What credit is to be given to this account of a
compromiſe of all the colonies will be evident
from governour Bernard's letter, dated in 1763,
which this ſpeaker cites, in confirmation of what
he hath ſaid. " At the time of making the mo-
" laſſes act, now thirty years ago, it was aſſerted
" by the Weſt Indians, that as the Britiſh Weſt
" Indian plantations were capable of taking off all
" the produce of America, the ſending ſuch pro-
" duce to foreign plantations ought to be diſ-
" couraged. To this the North Americans then
" anſwered, by denying (I believe with greater
" truth) that the Britiſh plantations were incapable
" of taking off all the produce of North Ame-
" rica fit for the Weſt India markets. The Weſt
" Indians prevailed, and a duty of 50 per cent.
" was laid by parliament on all molaſſes imported
" from iſlands not belonging to Great-Britain."

Was this act made, in conſequence of a *compromiſe*, which by that *exceſſive* duty on molaſſes,
not of the produce of the Britiſh iſlands, would
have ruined the North American trade, had it not
been evaded by contraband ? would the Americans,
on ſo intereſting an occaſion, have paid no attention
to the *new words* of *giving and granting*, had theſe
terms been exceptionable ; or had any doubt been

H 4 entertained

entertained of the right of the Britifh legiflature, to lay what taxes they thought proper on the colonies ? do not facts eternally arife to confute this orator in all his affertions ? and when he quotes the preceding letter of governor Bernard, who gives his opinion, not as the orator cites it, " that " it *was* an act of *prohibition* not of revenue," but that he *believes* it was originally defigned for a prohibition. But fuppofe it were, in what fenfe does that circumftance alter the meaning of the terms, *give and grant*, or anfwer the intention of this orator, when he afferts they were *premeditately* avoided for more than a century ?

" This," fays he, " is certainly true, that no " act avowedly for the purpofe of revenue, and " with the ordinary title and recital, *taken together*, " is found in the ftatute book until the year he " hath mentioned, that is in the year 1764." What a futile and obvious evafion of the reality of things is here intended! the *title* and *recital* are not in the *fame* act. But are they not feparately in diftinct acts ? if they are not, will not his own opinion, in one place, counterbalance it in another ? " that a *form of words* does not alter the nature of " the law, nor abridge the power of the law- " giver." To what intent then is all this *parlaver* about the form of words fo *lafhingly* and fo *naufeatingly* urged ?

" The fcheme of a colony revenue, by Britifh " authority, appeared therefore to the Americans " in the light of a great innovation ; the words of " governor Bernard's ninth letter, written in No- " vember 1765, ftates this idea very ftrongly. " It muft, fays he, have been fuppofed, *fuch an* " *innovation as a parliamentary taxation*, would " caufe a great *alarm*, and meet with much *op-* _

pofition,

" *position,* in moſt parts of America ; it was *quite*
" *new* to the people, and had no *viſible bounds* ſet
" to it. After ſtating the weakneſs of government
" there, he ſays, was this a time to introduce *ſo*
" *great a novelty,* as a parliamentary inland tax-
" ation in America ? whatever the right might
" have been, this mode of uſing it was abſolutely
" new in policy and practice."

If this orator be poſſeſſed of any degree of merit, it lies in its being undiſcoverable, whether his
aſſertions originate from ſheer ignorance, intended
falacy, or premeditated miſchief. By the antecedent quotation of governor Bernard's letter, it
is manifeſt he deſigned to create a perſuaſion in
you, that it related ſolely to the act paſſed in 1764,
relative to the preceding act of George the ſecond,
which laid ſo vaſt a duty on molaſſes imported
from other iſlands than the Britiſh. It is this act,
which he would induce you to believe, was that
which was conſidered as an innovation of a *par-*
liamentary taxation, that would cauſe an *alarm* ;
meet with much *oppoſition* ; be *quite new* to the
people ; and which had no *viſible bounds* ſet to it.
Yet ſuch is the fact, that all the preceding cir-
cumſtances have no more relation to the act of
1764, than to the firſt chapter of the Alcoran.
On the paſſing of that act, they never diſputed
the legiſlative authority. They thought of no innovation, and made no oppoſition to it. On the
contrary, in the 5th letter of governor Bernard,
the people of the Maſſachuſets petitioned parliament for redreſs from that duty, and from ſeveral
other things contained in that act. And by that
application, it was fully evinced, that they acknowledged the authority by which that act was
made. Every ſyllable, that this orator hath thus
applied to the act of 1764, ſtands in governor
Ber-

Bernard's letter, which he quotes, expreffive of
the ftamp-act only of 1765, the mention of which
he conceals. And thus he infidioufly reprefents the
former, "as the *great novelty of a parliamentary*
" *external taxation in America,*" although all the
antecedent circumftances are relative to an *internal*
taxation on paper. And then he fays, " what-
" ever the right might have been, this mode of
" ufing it was abfolutely new in policy and prac-
" tice ;" although it were as old in both as the
reign of Charles the fecond, which he himfelf allows.
If this be the refult of ignorance, can he for the
future be confidered as a man of common underftanding ? if it be the effect of an intended falacy,
at what rate fhall his integrity be eftimated? if it
be the confequence of premeditated mifchief,
what will you think of his heart? if a combination
of them all, what ——I will not afk the queftion.
" He now thinks the commercial reftraint is full
" as hard a law for the Americans to live under,
" as that for the American revenue, if uncom-
" penfated he thinks it to be a condition of as
" egregious fervitude as men can be fubject to.
" But America bore it from the fundamental act
" of navigation until 1764." To which I will
add until 1765. And fo fhe would have done to this
hour, if the enemies of this kingdom had not incenfed the colonifts to rebellion.

But not contented with affertions, he will give
you his reafons, and thus overfet on the other fide
what might have ftood, for a fhort time, had he
been lefs bufy in propping it. "Why?" his anfwer is,
" becaufe men do bear the inevitable conftitution
" of their original nature with all its infirmities."
And what infirmities either originally natural, or
adventitious do men *not bear*, which are *inevitable?* what a precious circumlocution of no meaning

ing, do the preceding words exhibit. The inference however is admirable. Becaufe thofe men
who have, by nature, hump-backs, bandy-legs,
patriotic eyes, or other infirmities of their *bodily
conftitutions*, which they cannot avoid, do bear
them; the Americans bore the navigation act,
which was a *hump* in their political conftitution,
until 1764, when they attempted to be *freed*
from what was *inevitably* to *hold them*.   This
if uncompenfated, he thinks as rigorous a fervitude as men can be fubject to. God fend us all, fay
I, erect poftures, ftraight limbs, and eyes unlike
the immaculate Lord Mayor, or the lord have mercy
on us! for otherwife, being thus prepared in body,
our *minds* will inevitably bear flavery of courfe.
Paddy Blake's echo would have given a more rational anfwer to that *why*; for when any one cried
aloud *how do you do captain Blake*, the echo very fen-
fibly anfwered for the captain, *pretty well I thank
you*. From the preceding paffage, it appears, that
the navigation act, which a few pages before " was
" the corner ftone of our policy, with regard to
" the colonies," is now become an infirmity in
that very policy.

After a fhort *exclamation* on the act of navigation, which, with its *infirmities*, " grew with their
" growth, and *ftrengthened* with their *ftrength*," he
talks of their monopolift, his riches, his immenfe
" capital, which primarily employed for his own
" benefit, enriched the others, and was a hot-
" bed to them ;" he adds, " nothing in the hif-
" tory of mankind is like their progrefs.   For his
" part, he never cafts an eye on their flourifhing
" commerce," under a monopoly, " their culti-
" vated commodious life," under a ftate of flavery.   " But they feem to him rather antient nation

" tions grown to perfection through a long feries
" of fortunate events, and a train of fucceſsful in-
" duſtry, accumulating wealth in many centuries,
" than the colonies of yeſterday; than a ſet of
" miſerable out-caſts, a few years ago, not ſo much
" ſent as thrown out on the bleak and barren ſhore
" of a deſolate wilderneſs, three thouſand miles
" from all civilized intercourſe."

I ſhall withhold my remarks on the happy ſtate
of the Americans for a few minutes. In the mean
while, I readily agree with this orator, that ſuch
a ſet of *miſerable outcaſts*, part rebels, part felons,
were thrown *out* from hence, and *into* the Maſſachuſets and Virginia; that the bleakeſt and moſt
barren ſhore of the moſt deſolate wilderneſs upon
earth, would have been too good and too hoſpitable
a retreat for them. "All this," he ſays, " was
" done by England, whilſt England purſued trade
" and forgot revenue." Since the revolution at
leaſt, I think that *revenue* has not been forgotten,
in this kingdom. And as England has created the
commerce, enriched the coloniſts, and made them
ſo happy, does it not ſeem reaſonable that a revenue ſhould now be thought on for America?
perhaps the ſubſequent paſſage of your orator may
juſtify ſuch a proceeding. " He ſays, we not only
" acquired commerce, but actually created the
" very objects of trade in America, and by that
" creation raiſed the trade of this nation at leaſt
" four-fold. America had the compenſation of
" your capital, which made her bear her ſervi-
" tude." Hence it appears, that no mother was
ever more indulgent to her progeny, than Britannia
to her colonies. It *created* the objects of their commerce; it ſupported them with her capital; and if
the trade of this kingdom was encreaſed four-fold,
by theſe means, was it not owing to herſelf; and
you

you have already seen from the words of this orator, how rapidly the Americans advanced to a cul-
tivated and commodious life, and attained a degree of accumulated wealth, to which antient nations arrived but through a long series of fortunate
events, and a train of successful industry. If this
unexampled progress to ease and happiness, whilst
you have been oppressed by debts, and burthened
with taxes, be a state of *servitude*, make me a
slave! give me the *effects!* let others find felicity
in the *sound* of liberty.

He persists " she had another compensation
" which you are now going to take from her.
" She had, except the commercial restraint, every
" characteristic mark of a free people in all her
" external and internal concerns. She had the
" image of the British constitution. She had the
" substance. She was taxed by her own repre-
" sentatives. She chose most of her own ma-
" gistrates. She paid them all. She had in effect
" the sole disposal of her own internal govern-
" ment." All these she would have still preserved, had she obeyed the law which imposed the
duties on the importation of the commodities already mentioned. All these circumstances are
correlative with those of all the cities and towns
corporate in England. They are charteral rights,
subordinate to the supreme legislative authority."
And do these rights take from the constituents, of
the respective corporations, any the minutest part,
of their liberty, because they are still obedient to
the laws of parliament? By what change in the
nature of things can the same cause reduce the colonists to *servitude*, which has been constantly
deemed a productive of *freedom* in England?
America still possesses the same image, the same
                                                    substance

fubftance of the Britifh conftitution, which you
enjoy. And on what account rebellion and ingratitude fhould be prefented with *more*, is a queftion
not eafily to be difcerned by loyal fubjects.

His obfervations are equal to all the other ex-
ertions of his intellect. He tells you " this *whole*
" ftate, of commercial *fervitude*, and civil *liberty*,
" taken together, is certainly not *perfect freedom*."
Which is as fhrewd a remark as that a magpye
being part *white* and part *black*, taken together is
not *all white*. " But, he adds, " comparing it
" with the ordinary circumftances of human na-
" ture, it was a happy and a liberal condition."
Such is the conclufion of his account of American
fervitude ; exactly like the *freedom* of Britons, a
happy and a *liberal* condition. A condition which
this orator, and his adherents, firft taught thefe Americans the infolence to queftion, the hardinefs to de-
fpife, and the madnefs to forfeit by rebellion. Thefe
are the bleffings for which the colonifts are obliged
to thofe, who wearing the patriotic mafk of faving
them, have at once involved their country and
her colonies in this unnatural contention.

" He knows," he tells you, " that great, and
" not unfuccefsful, pains have been taken to in-
" flame our minds, by an outcry, in this houfe
" and out of it, that in America the act of navi-
" gation neither is, nor never was obeyed. But
" as an anfwer to this," he affirms, " its authority
" never was difputed." If he *difobeyed* the ten
commands, does he imagine, that his not *dif-
puting* the *authority* which promulged them, will
be taken as a proof of his *obedience* to what they
injoin ? that would be an admirable and an eafy
method of attoning for fins. In fact, he confiders
his affirmation as an *anfwer* to his *own* pofition.

However,

However, to be always confiftent with himfelf, in the fubfequent words he fays, " that the autho-
" rity which was *never* difputed, was no where
" difputed for any *length* of time, and on the
" whole that it was well obferved." Thus it turns out, that what was *never difputed,* was neverthelefs *difputed,* but not *long.* How well it was ob-
ferved, his fucceeding words will convince you.
" Whenever the act preffed hard, many of the in-
" dividuals indeed evaded it. Thefe fcattered in-
" dividuals, never denied the law, and never
" obeyed it." This is certainly an excellent proof of laws being *well* obeyed, becaufe many individuals *evaded* it. Is it not an admirable and ju-
dicious affertion. " That the breach of the laws
" is nothing." What a number of individuals have been innocently executed at Tyburn for com-
mitting Mr. Burke's *nothing !* Is it not a pity that he is not minifter, to repeal thofe cruel acts which fend fuch a multiplicity of guiltlefs men to death, for doing nothing at all ? To the forego-
ing he adds, that " thefe fcattered individuals
" never obeyed the law, and never denied it."
And thus by way of difproof of what had been faid in the houfe, that the navigation act was *never obeyed,* he afferts that its *authority* was *never difputed,* although it was *fometimes* difputed : and that the law was *well* obeyed upon the whole, al-
though it was *difobeyed* by thofe on whom it preffed hard. And thofe you fhall prefently fee were the whole commercial fubjects of America. Thus, by way of apology for his American favourites, he allows that they never difputed the legiflative authority which enacted that law, but refufed to comply with it ; that is, they were not *miftaken* in their *judgments,* but *rogues* by *inclination,* in which
they

they perfift to this hour. The whole of this paffage is a piece of logical induction, fo exquifitely curious and unprecedented, that it cannot but eftablifh his reputation as a reafoner beyond all poffibility of demolition. But fuch is the peculiarity of his nature, he cannot be fatisfied until he has adduced every proof which can refute what he himfelf has advanced. Accordingly, he fays, the "laws were not *better obeyed* in this kingdom, from "Portland Frith to the ifle of Wight," which affords a fair inference, undoubtedly, that they *were* obeyed in America. And that the other parts of this kingdom are not fmugglers. Altho' he has fo happily eftablifhed his affertion by arguments, he is neverthelefs refolved to fupport it by authority. "I take it for granted," fays he, "that the au-"thority of governor Bernard, in this point, is "indifputable. Speaking of thefe laws, as they "regarded that part of America, now in fo un-"happy a condition, he fays, *I believe they are no* "*where better fupported than in this province. I do* "*not pretend it is entirely free from a breach of thefe* "*laws; but that fuch a breach, if difcovered, is* "*juftly punifhed.*" But is this a proof that they are duly obeyed, becaufe the *breach* of them is juftly punifhed if it be difcovered?

But facts fpeak for themfelves. In the third letter of the fame governor, and on the fame fubject, he fays, "the publication of orders for the "ftrict execution of the molaffes act has caufed "a greater alarm than the taking Fort William "Henry did in the year 1757. The merchants "fay, there is an end of the trade of this pro-"vince; that it is facrificed to the Weft-Indian "planters; petitions from the trading towns have "been prefented to the general court; and a large "committee

" committee of both houses is fitting every day
" to prepare inftructions to their agents." If
the e laws were well obeyed, and none but *scatter-
ed* individuals evaded them, whence did this *univerfal* alarm arife, on their being *obliged* to pay the
duty? on what account did *all* the merchants pronounce the *trade* of that province to be at an end;
if, antecedent to that time, the law and the payment
of the duties had not been univerfally eluded?
Thus, in calling the evidence of governor Bernard to his aid, your Orator has' abfolutely confirmed the truth of that which he fet out to difprove. "That in America the Act of Navigation
" neither is; nor ever was obeyed."

He proceeds. " Whether you were right or
" wrong in eftablifhing the colonies on the prin-
" ciples of commercial monopoly, rather than on
" that of revenue, is, at this day, a problem of
" mere fpeculation. You cannot have both by the
" fame authority. To join together the reftraints
" of an univerfal internal and external monopo-
" ly, with an univerfal internal and external taxa-
" tion, is an unnatural union; perfect uncompen-
" fated flavery. You have long fince decided for
" yourfelf and them; and you and they have
" profpered exceedingly under that decifion."

With refpect to the fpeculative problem I have
nothing to fay. But in order to place his affertion,
that we cannot have what he denominates a commercial monopoly, and a revenue by the fame authority, it is expedient that this monopoly be explained to you. To this intent it feems neceffary
to lay before you a fuccinct account of the American trade. It fhall be firft confidered relative to
the exportation from the colonies. All the iflands
belonging to Great Britain, in the Weft-Indies,

I   are

are open to the fale of whatever the American colonies do produce; and America, fouth of Florida, to that of their rice. 2. They trade to the Madeira and Azores iflands with their productions, from whence they carry back the wines of thofe countries. 3. All the parts of Europe, fouth of Cape Finiftre, are open to them for fifh, lumber, rice, grain, flour, and fugars of foreign growth. 4. To the north of that cape, their commerce is prohibited, without firft arriving in fome port of Great Britain. Tobacco, indico, furs, hemp, filk, turpentine, mafts, yards, &c. are to be landed in Great Britain only. Can this be deemed an univerfal monopoly refpecting this kingdom? But the word monopoly implies no kind of injuftice, if the effects of it be not injurious to thofe whom it excludes. Let me examine whether the preceding injunctions be to the benefit or difadvantage of the colonifts. The colonies in America, on a medium, are not lefs than three thoufand miles from Britain; and from fome of the ports on the northern and fouthern fhores of the European continent, they are much further. In all commercial intercourfe, nothing is more neceffary and advantageous, than the means of fpeedily tranfmitting intelligence from one place to another. Letters from Britain, or from any of the preceding ports, cannot be conveyed to America, and anfwers received in lefs than three months, on a medium. And this inevitable circumftance is attended with fuch manifeft inconveniencies, that it may be eftimated at an almoft impracticability of correfpondence. The confequences which muft arife from this delay and uncertainty, are fometimes crouded markets, which reduce the prices of their commodities; at others, the lofs of profit by being
uninformed

uninformed of the proper times of sending them. Besides other incidents, which are sufficiently obvious to mercantile men. In such cafes, and at such distances, an *interport* for lodging the American productions becomes absolutely necessary. And if the laws did not require the commodities, above-mentioned, to be landed and lodged in England, the interest of the colonists would have obliged them to fix on such an intermediate place. The merchants of England are factors for the colonists, to whom their productions are consigned. These have a quick and certain correspondence with the merchants of other European nations. They are timely acquainted with the rise and fall of their prices ; can sell them or not, according to their intelligence and judgement. The interests of the colonists and of their factors are the same. The height of the price is the benefit of both ; of the former in the sale, and of the latter in his per *cents*. And as the duties, either paid, or for which bonds have been given, are, on export, either repaid or remitted, the expences which arise from commissions are more than compensated by a degree of profit, which could not be otherwise obtained. Such being the state of that which, as I suppose, your orator calls an external monopoly, what injury is hereby done to the Americans? are not you the inhabitants of this kingdom in a worse situation? are there not many of your productions, the export of which is absolutely interdicted? such as sheep, wool, wool-fells, yarn of wool, fuller's earth, and others; but is this to be deemed a monopoly, because the national welfare requires that they shall not be sold to others?

With respect to the monopoly of internal commerce, I suppose it may mean, a pro-

hibition

hibition of one colony from sending their manu-
factured hats and a few other things into the
others; and that of permitting none but British
manufactures, or such merchandize as hath been
landed in Britain, provisions from Ireland excepted, to be imported into America. But when
it is considered that, of all the manufactures and
commodities produced in this kingdom, which pay
either excise or duty, and most others imported
into it, such as Portugal and Spanish wines, East-
India and other goods, the duties are drawn back
on exportation to America; that premiums are
given to encourage them to the producing of a
variety of commodities, which they otherwise
would not attempt, and by these means to get your
money; and bounties on some of our exported merchandize, which reduces the prices below what you pay; when they are consumed
by you, certainly there can be nothing either
destructive or unjust, respecting the Americans,
in such a monopoly. Are not you, the inhabitants of this kingdom, subjected to like conditions? can you trade where you please, and
import what you like? neither velvets nor wrought
silks, silk stockings and gloves, lawns, gold and
silver lace, cloths, several forts of iron, and other
wares, can be imported by you; and on other
commodities the duties are so great, that they
amount to a prohibition, but to such as are in
opulence. Besides these, you are under the restraints of monopolies, which rescind you from
the rights of trading to several parts of the globe;
such as those of the East-India, the Turky, and
the Hudson's bay company.

The

The same authority however which established all these commercial restraints in Britain, hath in like manner imposed an internal taxation on land, on light, on most of the necessaries of life by actual duties, and eventually on all, before they come to the consumer. Whence, therefore, does it arise; from what principle or precedent in polity does he affirm; that the legislative authority, which has constitutionally effected all these things in Britain, cannot effect the like purposes in America? or from what circumstances does it spring, that the colonies, into which, as he allows, trade hath overflowed with such redundance of riches, should be unable to afford such taxes as are necessary for their own occasions; whilst you are bound to furnish those for England which are so enormous?

If such be the *state* of England respecting commerce and taxation, according to Mr. Burke it must be a perfect uncompensated *slavery*. And yet under this slavery you have been happy. The foreign trade of your country and the balance of it have amazingly encreased. For in the year 1718, that balance was but 1,585,912*l*. and in 1764, it amounted to 6,179,808*l*. of which balance, the magnified trade of America produced about one seventh. As *you* have increased in wealth, and proceeded in felicity under this authority, what argument can be adduced that the same authority cannot effect the like ends in America? are you to remain content with labouring for the Americans, whilst they untaxed, unless they please, shall revel in a cheap abundance, deride your follies, and renounce that authority which, as subjects, they are bound to obey?

I 3 He

He now adds, " the nation never thought of
" departing from that choice (relative to America)
" until the period immediately on the close of the
" last war. Then a scheme of government, new
" in many things, seemed to have been adopted.
" He saw, or thought he saw, several symptoms
" of a great change whilst he sat in the gallery,
" a good while before he had the honour of a seat
" in that house." Or ever thought that honour would be his. Oh what a day was that, for
Britain's glory, when Edmund Burke was first entrusted with your rights and liberties! without that
vast event, the world had never seen this *speech*.

" At that period, says he, the necessity was
" established of keeping up no less than twenty
" new regiments, with twenty colonels, capable
" of seats in this house. This scheme was adopted
" with very general applause from all sides, at the
" very time, that by your conquests in America,
" your danger from foreign attempts, in that part
" of the world, was much lessened, or indeed
" quite over."

In what manner the *parliament* could *establish* a
necessity of keeping up these regiments seems not
to be easily understood. But that the *necessity* of
circumstances should induce the parliament to such
an *establishment* is within the reach of comprehension. As Hercules traced the oxen into the cave of
Cacus, by proceeding contrary to their footsteps ;
so the words of this gentleman are to be taken
in the inverted order. And thus it happens, that
the tricks of a thief, and the wiles of an orator may be discovered by observing a similar in-
vestigation. Whatever he might think he saw,
when he sat in the gallery, it seems sufficiently
clear, he did not discern that the reason for this
military

military eftablifhment was that which he confiders as rendering fuch an eftablifhment ufelefs; the Americans having nothing to fear from *foreign* attempts, as the Canadians were then become the fubjects of this realm. It was forefeen, however, by the miniftry, that this very circumftance of, the Americans having no fuch enemy to fear, would require a military force to oblige them to that duty which they owe the fovereign authority : more efpecially as the democratic fpirit of the Americans, inftigated by the infolence of accumulated riches, would inevitably return to the exercife of their native oppofition to this government. Thefe were the *circumftances*, and not the parliament, which *eftablifhed* the *neceffity* of an army. As to the twenty colonels, who were then made, and capable of feats in parliaments, does he imagine that men of that rank may not be as fafely intrufted with the liberties of their country; and be as free from corrupt influence, as a private clerk to a minifter, who may have nothing to *lofe* but his place?

I pafs the remarks on " the country gentleman, " thefe patrons of œconomy, and refifters of a " ftanding armed force, who adopted this fcheme " with fo much applaufe, and haften to Mr. " Townfhend, who, in a brilliant harangue, did " *dazzle* the commons, by playing before their " eyes the *image* of a *revenue* to be raifed in Ame- " rica." To *dazzle* by an *image* is undoubtedly excellent; but when by profopopœia, he gives *perfonality* to *revenue*, and then makes her *dazzling image*, it is incomparable. However, it imparts no bad idea of Mr. Townfhend's commencing fhowman, and playing a puppet; and the houfe fitting as fpectators and applauding him.

Not

Not content with the display of his parts and acquirements in the antecedent subjects, he now deviates from that narrative into the characters of men. In this part you shall see, that the same vanity, the same degree of knowledge, the same preservation of verisimilitude, are exhibited, as in those which he has already delivered. Mr. Grenville is the first minister whom he presumes to delineate. He, it seems, " with no small study " of the detail, did not seem to have his view, " at least, equally carried to the total circuit of " our affairs; he generally considered his objects " in lights that were too detached." And thus he begins this exhibition of his skill in characters with a refinement in observation, that a man who saw things in *detail* and in *detached* lights, did *not* carry his view to the *total* circuit of affairs. As well might he have said that a short-sighted person does not see at a great distance. And then he adds, " Mr. Grenville was of a masculine under- " standing," which does not delight in the study of detail, nor is engaged in the contemplation of de- tached objects. And thus two irreconcilable characte- ristics, that of attending to the most minute, and to the most extensive objects, are united in the same intellect. Conditions which are as incompatible in the *mind* of man, as that his *body*, chopped into bits, should be nevertheless entire.

He continues his pourtrait. "Mr. Grenville was " bred in a profession, he was bred in the law, " which is, in his opinion, one of the first and " noblest of human sciences, a science which does " more to quicken and invigorate the understand- " ing, than all the other kinds of learning put " together; but it is not apt, except in persons " very happily born, to open and liberalize the
" mind

" mind exactly in the fame proportion." Thus,
according to this picture-drawer, Mr. Grenville
" with a mafculine underltanding, a ftout and refolute heart, a firft-rate figure in this country, with
an ambition to fecure to himfelf a well earned rank
in parliament, by a thorough knowledge of its
conftitution, and a perfect practice in all its bufinefs, and with an application undiffipated and unwearied, was neverthelefs fo unhappily born, that
his mind could not be opened and liberalized by
the law, in exact proportion to the extenfivenefs of
thefe qualities," which feems to be fomewhat extraordinary. But that was not the whole caufe of
Mr. Grenville's being the inadequate man, which
this orator reprefents him. For, " paffing from
" that ftudy, he did not go very largely into the
" world, but plunged into bufinefs, he means
" into the bufinefs of office, and the limited and
" fixed methods of forms eftablifhed there." That
Mr. Grenville did not go very *largely into* the world,
nor *out* of it either, is certainly true ; for he lived
and died extremely *meagre.* But if he mean
largely in a figurative fenfe, he is certainly miftaken. His birth, his connections, his company
evince the reverfe of that affertion. And into what
other place could a man, with all the preceding
talents, quickened and invigorated by the fcience
of the law, have gone with more propriety in his
progrefs to the prime miniftry, than into office ?
was it not in that fituation that he could inftruct
himfelf in the fixed methods and forms eftablifhed
for carrying the conceptions of a mafculine underftanding and a refolute heart into execution ?

He now recovers a little from this difadvantage
of office, in which he has placed Mr. Grenville,
and adds, " much knowledge is to be had un-
" doubtedly

" doubtedly in that line ; and there is no *know-*
" *ledge* which is not *valuable.*" An obfervation as
acute as that of a *Welch* juryman, who told the
judge, if the culprit was *hanged*, his life would be
in *great danger*. Again he deviates from the merit
of that official knowledge, and fays, " that men
" too converfant in office, are rarely minds of re-
" markable enlargement ; their habits of office are
" apt to give them a turn to think the fubftance
" of bufinefs not to be much more important than
" the forms in which it is conducted. Thefe
" forms are adapted to ordinary occafions ; and
" therefore perfons who are nurtured in office, do
" admirably well, as long as things go on in the
" common order ; but when the high roads are
" broken up and the waters out, when a new and
" troubled fcene is opened, and the file affords
" no precedent, then it is a greater knowledge of
" mankind, and a far more extenfive *comprehen-*
" *fion* of things is requifite than ever office gave,
" or than office can ever give.

Such is his delineation of Mr. Grenville. In-
confiftencies in fome degree are probably to be
found in the characters of all men ; but moral impoffibilities in none. Such as a *mafculine underftand-*
ing, miftaking the *form* for the *fubftance*. A *ftout*
and *refolute heart*, that was *not* fit to *encounter* difficulties ; a *quickened* and *invigorated* underftanding, adapted to nothing but *ordinary* occafions ;
a *noble ambition*, and an *unwearied application*,
which had made him *no more* than a *clerk* in office. It is a common artifice of bad painters to
caricature the features of their pourtraits, in order
to make the likeneffes more ftriking. But this
gentleman draws not from nature, but from a
fancy, that in all things conjoins fuch particulari-
ties,

ties, whether intellectual or substantial, as never can exist in the same object. In this examination of Mr. Grenville's character, I pretend not to distinguish how far your orator is in the right or mistaken, respecting some perticular parts separately taken. All I would prove is, that they never did, nor ever can exist in the same person, and therefore that he is absolutely unskilled in the science of human-kind.

I beg one moment's leave to return to Mr. *Grenville*, for the sake of exhibiting Mr. Burke. "No "man can believe," says he, "that *I* mean to "*lean* upon Mr. Grenville's memory." By which I imagine he means to *bear hard* upon it. " Our "little party differences have been long ago com- "posed; and *I* have acted more with him, than "ever *I* acted against him." *Party-differences*, and *actings* with and against Mr. Grenville, first lord of the Treasury, and chancellor of the Exchequer, by Edmund Burke, clerk to Lord Rockingham, by the curtesy of England called secretary, as every man now is, who knotches at the kiln, an account of bricks on a stick, to him who transacts the business of the state. Does he consider his *verbosity* to be *action*? In what other way could he act, either with or against Mr. Grenville? Should Robert Mackreith, Esq; at the end of this session of parliament, talk of acting with or against Edmund Burke, Esq; in his votes, with what profound indignation would the latter resent so offensive a familiarity of expression! and yet honest Bob was *secretary* to Lord Rockingham, and to a number of other lords at the same time; whilst Mr. Burke was *high in air*, meditating on the sublime and beautiful, equally as unsuspecting and unspected of ever becoming a member of

par-

parliament, as Mr. Mackreith, his brother fecretary, or Rumbold, who was Mackreith's.

I pafs now to his defcription of the trade of
America. " After the war, and in the laft years
" of it, the trade of America had encreafed far
" beyond the fpeculations of the moft languine
" imagination ; it fwelled *out* on every fide. It
" *filled* its proper channels to the *brim*. It *over-*
" *flowed* with a rich redundance, and *breaking* its
" *banks* on the *right* and on the *left* ; it fpread out
" oh fome places where it was indeed improper
" upon others where it was only irregular." The
preceding imagery is taken from a river fwoln
with ruins. And as in the character of Mr. Grenville, he hath combined moral impoffibilities, fo in
this he hath united natural. The trade fwells *out* on
every *fide*, and yet the *channels* are but *brimful*.
It *overflows* its *banks*, and yet it *breaks them down*.
Here is indeed an overflowing redundance of
founding words and foaming contradictions, and
as Major O'Flaharty fays, a very plentiful fcarcity
of every thing elfe.

He then tells you " it is the nature of all great-
" nefs not to be exact." If the greatnefs of his
oratory be in proportion to his *want* of exactnefs
in this fpeech, then muft every orator, ancient and
modern, yield in greatnefs to Edmund Burke,
Efq; and he has fixed a monument more durable
than brafs. In whom is there to be found fuch
amazing *marks* of fuch *greatnefs? words* without *ideas ;*
affirmation againft *facts ; conclufions* which the *pre-*
mifes deny ; animal vivacity without *imagery*, *rea-*
foning without *logic*, and *arguments* which *difprove*
the things they are intended to *eftablifh*. Such
is the redundant want of exactnefs which fhall fix
him in an eternal permanency of greatnefs ; whilft
that

that of speakers, founded on the opposite qualifications, shall, like the baseless fabric of a vision, dissolve, and leave no wreck behind.

It is his laudable ambition to be constantly exhibiting some new excellence, in the exertion of his intellectual faculties. He now imitates the great Rochefaucault, and turns maxim-maker. " It " should stand," says he, " as a fundamental " maxim, that no vulgar precaution ought to be " employed in the cure of evils, which are closely " connected with the cause of our prosperity." *Maxims* have hitherto been considered as a species of *self evident truths*, and *easily* to be put in *practice*. But this *maxim* is in its first part impracticable; and in the second repugnant to common-sense. For by what means can a *precaution*, an act which can only *prevent*, be employed to *cure* an *evil* which is actually *existing*? But let the *hereditary right* of this orator be acknowledged. Let it be supposed, that by *precaution*, which can only be used *before* the evil arrives, he would signify the *means* of curing it *after* it has happened. This metaphor is derived from his knowledge in the art of healing. For of him alone it can be truly said, *he is equally instructed in all things.* I will ask him therefore, if a person inflicted with an ague, or the venereal disease, should consult him, would he abstain from curing them by the bark and mercury, because they are vulgar means; and leave the evil closely connected with his patient's health, because he had no uncommon remedy to effect a cure? If a mortification had seized a limb, or a wen grew on the body of a person, must the surgeon abstain from amputation, because it is the vulgar means of cure; and leave these two evils closely connected with the body?

body ? And now I defire to know, on what this *fundamental maxim* can *ftand*, that *never* can or ought to *exift* ?

He then tells you, " Mr. Grenville perhaps turned his eye fomewhat lefs than was juft, to the " *incredible* encreafe of their fair trade, and looked " with fomething of too inquifitive a jealoufy to- " wards the contraband; and that the bonds of " the act of navigation were ftraitened fo much, " that America was on the point of having no " trade, either contraband or *legitimate.*" By which I fuppofe he means *lawful.*

I come now to what your orator ftiles " the " grand manœuvre in the bufinefs of regulating " the colonies. It was the 15th act of the fourth " of George the third, which, befides containing " feveral of the matters to which he hath juft be- " fore alluded, opened a new principle : and here " properly began the fecond period of the policy " of this country with regard to the colonies ; by " which the fcheme of a regular plantation par- " liamentary was adopted in theory, and fettled " in practice, a revenue not fubftituted in place " of, but fuperadded to a monopoly, was enforced " at the fame time with additional ftrictnefs, and " the execution put into military hands."

"This act had, *for the firft time, the title of grant-* " *ing duties in the colonies and plantations of America,* " and for the firft time it was afferted in the pre- " amble, that it was *juft* and *neceffary* that a re- " venue fhould be raifed there. Then came the " technical words of *giving and granting* ; and thus " a complete American revenue act was made in " all the forms, and with a full avowal of the " right, equity, and policy, and even neceffity of " of taxing the colonies, with any formal confent of theirs. He

He has already told you, that " a form of
" words alters not the nature of the law, nor
" abridges the power of the law-giver." I shall
therefore say no more respecting the title. But
was it not *just* and *necessary* that a revenue should
be raised in America ? *Just*, because their trade
was so *incredibly* encreased, and flowing over with
a rich redundance. *Necessary*, because, in defence
of those colonies, this nation is incumbered with a
debt of seventy millions? As to the *right* of taxing them, he not only avows that it had been exer-
cised from the reign of king Charles the 2d; but *be
advised*, and his minister obtained an act declaratory of the parliamentary right to tax them, without *qualification*. In these circumstances, did not
equity to you, the subjects of this realm, demand
that the Americans should be taxed in alleviation
of the oppressions which you bear ? Was it not
true policy in the minister, to consider your state
and prepare to improve it ? and did not these circumstances create a *necessity* of taxing the colonies ?
As to their consent, it never had been asked in
former acts of taxation. Could the legislature imagine the consent of the Americans necessary to form
a British statute ? Had they deviated into that mistake, they had subverted the constitution of this
realm, by considering the colony assemblies as part
of the supreme legislature ? Had his majesty, by
his ministers, made a requisiton of supplies, he
had extended his prerogative to a degree of annihilating the parliamentary authority in America;
his ministers had been traitors; and an ignominious death had been the just reward of their treachery to the state. Do not these circumstances
afford an indisputable testimony of the *right*, *equity*,
policy, and *necessity* of such an act, and an ample
justi-

juftification of Mr. *Grenville*'s fyftem of raifing a revenue on the Americans?

But it feems the preamble contained thefe remarkable words. " The Commons, &c. being " defirous to make *fome* provifion in the *prefent* " feffion of parliament, *towards* raifing the faid " revenue." And in your reprefentatives, whofe indifpenfible duty it is to alleviate the burthen of your taxes; was it not a juft defire, which ought to be carried into execution? But can the *defire* of parliament, to make *fome* provifion in the *then* feffion, *towards* raifing a revenue, authorife this fpeaker to affert, " that it appeared to the co- " lonies, that this act was the beginning of for- " row; that every feffion was to produce fomething " of the fame kind; that the parliament was to " go on from day to day, in charging them with " fuch taxes as they pleafed; for fuch a military " force as they fhould think proper." And what is there in all this, more than is conftitutionally done, in this kingdom, every feffion of parliament? And where he tells you, " the execution of the " act was put into military hands," if he mean that the army was to collect the tax, he knows he utters an untruth, with malevolence prepenfe to inflame you against the miniftry. In one moment you fhall fee him contradict this behaviour of the Americans and himfelf.

" Had this plan been purfued," fays he, " it " was evident that the provincial affemblies, in " which the Americans felt all their portion of " importance, and beheld their fole image of " freedom, were *ipfo facto* annihilated." It feems probable, that the corporation of London is more ancient than the exiftence of a houfe of Commons, and there is no certainty when it was firft inftituted,

being

being by prefcription antecedent to any fubfifting
charter. When the parliament took place, as it
now exifts, and the fupreme legiflative authority
laid duties on the Londoners, were " their por-
" tion of importance and fole image of freedom
" annihilated ?" Have they and the other incorporated bodies, hitherto conceived that fuch was the
effect of the *parliamentary power* being fuperior to
that of the charteral ? How then could this conftitutional authority offer " an ill profpect to the
" Americans that feemed boundlefs in extent, and
" endlefs in duration?" He tells you, however, "they
" were not miftaken." And what are the reafons
he adduces in proof that the profpect was boundlefs, and endlefs ? It was, becaufe " the miniftry
" valued themfelves when this act paffed, and
" when they gave notice of the ftamp act, that
" both of the duties came very far fhort of their
" ideas of American taxation." And then, on this
proof of the inefficacy of thefe taxes, he adds, great
" was the applaufe of thefe meafures here." Thus the
miniftry valued themfelves and were *applauded* for that
in which they had *mifcarried*. "In England, how-
" ever, we cried out for new taxes on America,
" whilft they cried out they were nearly crufhed
" with thofe which the war, and their own grants
" had brought upon them." And from thefe two
outcries, he has drawn thefe *conclufions,* that " the
Americans were *not miftaken.*" That " the American *importance,* and their *fole image of freedom*
were annihilated, and the *profpect* of being reduced
to nothing was become *boundlefs* in *extent,* and
endlefs in *duration.*"

When the mile ftones were firft erected on the
Oxford road, a village, that had been hitherto
reckoned to be *five,* was now found to be *feven*

K   miles

miles from that city. On this an old woman of
the village made a lamentable *outcry* againſt the
cruelty of the turnpike commiſſioners. For when
the road conſiſted but of *five miles*, ſaid ſhe, I
could walk very well to Oxford: but now they
have made it *ſeven*, I can go no more there. And
thus ſhe loſt her *portion* of *importance* and *ſole
image of freedom.* I do not infer from hence, that
this celebrated ſpeaker reaſons like an old woman ;
it is only to ſhew, that ſimilar geniuſes do frequently coincide in the manner of forming concluſions
from like premiſes.

He now tells you, " it has been ſaid in the de-
" bate, that when the firſt American revenue act
" (the act in 1764 impoſing the port duties).
" paſſed, the Americans did not object to the
" principle ; it is true they touched it but very
" gently. It was not a direct attack." And thus
this orator, reſtleſs until he hath demoliſhed his
own edifice, becomes an evidence againſt himſelf ; and amply teſtifies that the very act, which
he aſſerts, had given the proſpect, to the Americans, of their importance and their freedom being
annihilated, had " paſſed without any objection,
to the principle, or with a light touch only."
The reaſon is, " they did not conſider it as a direct
attack ;" and therefore they never could have fan-
cied any ſuch boundleſs proſpect, or eternity of
duration, as he mentions. And now, conſiſtent in
inconſiſtency alone, he aſſigns the reaſons why they
could *not* have had ſuch a proſpect ; " they were
" as yet novices ; as yet unaccuſtomed to direct
" attacks upon any of the rights of parliament.
" The duties were port duties, like thoſe they had
" been accuſtomed to bear, with this difference,
" that the title was not the ſame, the preamble not
" the

"" the fame, and the fpirit altogether unlike." And thus having depofed in contradiction to himfelf, he brings arguments to prove, that with all thefe additional circumftances, the duties were fuch as they were accuftomed to bear ; that therefore they had neither a right to object to the law, nor a motive to create that vifionary profpect which he defcribes, and that by now *firft attacking* the *rights* of *parliament*, they began their progrefs to rebellion.

He now afks, " of what fervice is this obferva-
" tion (*that the Americans did not object to the par-*
" *liament authority*) to the caufe of thofe that make
" it ? it is a full refutation for the pretence of
" their prefent cruelty to America ; for it fhews,
" out of their own mouths, that our colonies were
" backwards to enter into the prefent vexations
" and ruinous controverfy." From hence, it fhould appear, that the miniftry have made the *acquiefcence* of the Americans with the act of 1764, a *pretence* for their prefent cruelty, as he calls it. Otherwife how can that conduct, in the colonifts, be a refutation of that pretence ? but is that the cafe ? and when it fhews out of the miniftry's own mouths, that the colonies were backwards to enter into the prefent controverfy, does it not fhew alfo, out of the orator's, when they refift what they had *never* before *objected to*, that they rebelled againft their own convictions. And therefore they ought to be compelled to obey that parliamentary authority, which antecedently they never had oppofed, and now prefume *directly to attack ?*

He advances with equal fuccefs in the fubfequent affirmation. " There is alfo another cir-
" culation abroad (fpread with a malignant in-
" tention, which he cannot attribute to thofe who

K 2 " fay

" fay the fame thing in the houle) that Mr. Gren-
" ville gave the colony agents an option for their
" affemblies to tax themfelves, which they had
" refuled. He finds much ftrefs is laid on this as
" a fact. However, it happens neither to be true
" nor poffible." I fhall confront this hardy affertion by an evidence not to be refuted. It was
printed in the London Evening Poft, Feb. 28,
and fubfcribed *Ifrael Manduit.*

" In the beginning of March 1764, a number
" of refolutions, relative to the plantation trade,
" were propofed by Mr. Grenville, and paffed in
" the houfe of commons.—The fifteenth of thefe
" was, that towards the further defraying the
" faid expences, it may be proper to charge cer-
" tain ftamp duties on the faid colonies and plan-
" tations. The other refolutions were formed into
" the plantation act, and the fifteenth was put
" off till the next feffion, Mr. Grenville declaring
" that he was willing to give time to the colonies
" to confider of it, and to make their option of
" raifing that or fome other tax. The agents
" waited feparately on Mr. Grenville upon this
" matter, and wrote to their feveral colonies. At
" the end of the feffion, we went to him, all of
" us together, to know if he ftill intended to bring
" in fuch a bill; he anfwered, he did; and then
" repeated to us, in form, what I had heard
" him fay before in private; and in the houfe of
" commons; that the late war had found us feventy
" millions, and left us more than one hundred
" and forty millions in debt. He knew that all
" men wifhed not to be taxed; but that in their
" unhappy circumftances, it was his duty, as a
" fteward for the public, to make ufe of every
" juft means of improving the public revenue:
" that

" that he never meant, however, to charge the
" colonies with any part of the interest of the
" national debt. But besides that public debt,
" the nation had incurred a great annual expence
" in the maintaining of the several new conquests,
" which we had made during the war, and by
" which the colonies were so much benefited.
" That the American civil and military establish-
" ment, after the peace of Aix la Chapelle, was
" only 70,000l. per annum. It was now encreased
" to 350,000l. This was a great additional ex-
" pence incurred upon an American account:
" and he thought, therefore, that America ought
" to contribute towards it. He did not expect
" that the colonies should raise the whole, but
" some part of it he thought they ought to raise,
" and this stamp-act was intended for that pur-
" pose."

" That he judged this method of raising the
" money the easiest and most equitable; that it
" was a tax which would fall only upon property;
" would be collected by the fewest officers; and
" would be equally spread over America and the
" West-Indies; so that all would bear their share
" of the public burthen.

" He then went on, I am not however set upon
" this tax; if the Americans dislike it, and pre-
" fer any other method of raising the money
" themselves, I shall be content. Write therefore
" to your several colonies, and if they chuse any
" other mode, I shall be satisfied, provided the
" money be but raised."

This conversation was transmitted to the colonies,
by their agents, to which they received the following answers.

Boston,

Boston, June 14, 1754.

" Sir,

" The house of representatives have received
" your several letters, &c. The actual laying the
" stamp duty, you say, is deferred till next year.
" Mr. Grenville being willing to give the pro-
" vinces their option to raise that, or some other
" equivalent tax, desirous, as he was pleased to
" express himself, to consult the ease and quiet,
" and the good will of the colonies.——If the
" ease, the quiet, and the good will of the co-
" lonies are of any importance to Great Britain,
" no measure could be hit upon that hath a more
" natural and direct tendency to enervate those
" principles, than the resolutions you enclosed.
" The kind offer of suspending this stamp duty
" in the manner, and upon the condition you
" mention, amounts to no more than this: that
" if the colonies will not tax themselves, as they
" may be directed, the parliament will tax them.
" ——You are to remonstrate against these mea-
" sures, and, if possible, to obtain a repeal of
" the sugar act, and prevent the imposition of
" any further duties or taxes on the colonies :
" measures will be taken that you may be joined
" by all the other agents."

From hence it is evident, that Mr. Grenville did
indisputably propose to the colonies the raising of
a duty adequate to the purpose of the stamp-act ;
and that these refractory colonists did positively
refuse to accept that offer. Thus it is demon-
strated, that what this accurate orator pronounces
to be neither *true* nor *possible*, are *real facts*. After
this I shall not trouble you with refuting the
reasons which he brings to prove, that what did
certainly

certainly exift, had no *exiftence*. It is true, that the act of 1764 is, in your orator's account, fo blended with that of the ftamp-act of 1765, that it looks as if he had mixed them in this manner from a confcioufnefs of being open to immediate confutation without that artifice ; and by thefe means that he intended to efcape detection, like the ink fifh, which blackens the waters, and renders the fpot, in which he lies, invifible to his purfuers. Even the letter of governor Bernard, which he quotes, mult have convinced him, that the preceding propofal of Mr. Grenville was relative to the ftamp-act only ; but as he adduces this tranfcript as a proof, that the Americans, burthened as they were, were not then taxable; as it comes from a refpectable authority, it merits your confideration.
" The American governments had, in the pro-
" fecution of the late war, contracted very large
" debts, which it will take fome years to pay off,
" and in the mean time occafion very burdenfome
" taxes for that fupport only ; for inftance, this
" government (the Maffachufets) which is as much
" before-hand as any, raifes every year 37,500*l.*
" fterling, for finking their debt, and muft con-
" tinue it for four years longer at leaft, before it
" will be clear."

This inability founded on their debts, incurred in the laft war, which concluded with *happinefs, fecurity*, and *opulence* to them; is an argument, than which nothing can be more inconclufive. In this war undertaken for thefe Americans, this colony ran in debt 150,000*l.* which they can difcharge in *four years*; and you, of this kingdom, for their defence, incurred a debt of 70,000,000*l.* for the liquidation of which, the duration of the world will not allow a time fufficient. The intereft of

that

that immenfe fum, you, your children, and all
fucceeding generations, are mortgaged to pay, by
the fweat of your brows; whilft thefe traiterous
Americans, wantoning in eafe and opulence, refufe
to contribute to the payment of thofe taxes which
are requifite for the fupport of their own governments! Such is the object of their rebellious oppofition. Such is the boon, which this orator, and
their abettors are labouring to obtain for them!
and under the deceitful mafk of *patriotifm*, to *annihilate* the fupreme *rights* of their *own* country,
and by the *found* of *liberty* to oblige you inceffantly
to toil as *flaves* for traitors. It is their interelt,
their ambition, their luft of power, their private
ends, to which *thefe patriots* tend, under the often-
tatious pretext of *public virtue*. And now in the
words of your orator, I fhall fay, "thus I have
" difpofed of this falfehood;" but as he tells you,
" falfehood has a perennial fpring," I will, therefore, purfue him through the remainder of his
fpeech, and ftick to him like defperation to a na-
bob's confcience.

He now tells you, "it is faid, that no conjecture
" could be made of the diflike of the colonifts
" to the principle. This is as untrue as the
" other." It is precifely in the fame predicament,
and you fhall have the proof from himfelf; the
principle is the *legiflative authority*, and to *that authority*, refpecting the act of 1764, he has already
told you the Americans did not object. Whence
then could the conjecture arife, that they would
oppofe that *principle* in the *next* year, the *right* of
which they had *acknowledged* in the *former?* but
there is no neceffity of receding to his paft fayings
for a confutation of himfelf. The paffage which
immediately follows is adequate to that end.
" After

" After the resolution of the house," says he, "and
" before the passing of the stamp-act, the colonies
" of the Massachuset's Bay and New York did
" send remonstrances, objecting to this *mode* of
" parliamentary taxation." And thus he concludes, that the *principle*, the *legislative authority*,
is the same with the *laws* it makes, or the *mode* of
taxation; and therefore because the Americans disliked the thing *created*, they objected to the *creator*
also. Thus an *aversion* from a *toad* is a *dislike*
to the *deity*.

He then asks, " what was the consequence?
" The remonstrances were suppressed, they were
" put under the table, notwithstanding an order
" of council to the contrary, by the ministry which
" composed the very council that had made the
" order; and thus the house proceeded to its busi-
" ness of taxing, without the least regular know-
" ledge of the objections which were made to it."
Which is, if I understand this passage, that the house
of Commons ordered these remonstrances to be put
under the table, notwithstanding an order of council to keep them above board. A right which the
Commons ought to exert in opposition to all *orders*
of *council*. But the true reason was, that when the
house was acquainted with the true disposition of
the Americans, by their agents, and their own
letters; and that they were determined not to obey
the parliamentary authority, they acted as a British
senate, and every legislative authority ought to
act. They would not permit the sovereignty of
the realm to become a subject of debate, or called
in question. Such a proceeding would have pronounced them to be traitors to their trust and to
the state; besides the eternal objection of being
judges in their own cause. They therefore rightly
proceed

proceed to the bufinefs of taxing the Americans in
contempt of every objection, and the ftamp act
was paffed.

"This," fays he, "was the ftate of the colonies,
" before his majefty thought fit to change his mini-
" ftry; it ftands upon *no* authority of his." Indeed he
has no authority for what he has faid, and confequently the whole has no foundation, as it has been
fully proved by incontrovertible records. " Mr.
" Cornwall," he fays, " has defired fome of them
" to lay their hands upon their hearts, and anfwer
" to his queries upon the hiftorical part of this
" confideration, and by his manner he feemed to
" addrefs himfelf to him. He will anfwer him
" with great opennefs ; he has nothing to conceal."
By thus affuming to *himfelf* this addrefs of Mr.
Cornwall to *fome* of them, would you not imagine
that he had been chancellor of the Exchequer, or
leader of minifterial bufinefs in the houfe, during
the Rockingham adminiftration, whofe uprightnefs
had nothing to fear or to conceal ? But you fhall
hear what he fays of himfelf, with an account of
whom he begins the hiftorical part of this confideration, like *the memoirs of P. P. clerk of this
parifh.* " In the year fixty-five, being in a private
" ftation, far enough from any line of bufinefs,
" and not having the honour of a feat in this houfe,
" it was my fortune," fays he, " unknowing and
" unkown to the then miniftry, by the interven-
" tion of a common friend, to become connected
" with a very noble perfon, and at the head of the
" Treafury department." Fortunate to *him,* but
fatal to his *friend.* The deed hung heavy on his
foul. He———but I will proceed no further in
the relation of an event, by which we loft a man,
whofe

whofe fenfations were too delicate to bear the dif-
appointments of miftaken friendfhip.

" It was," he adds, " indeed in a fituation of
" little rank, and no confequence, fuitable to the
" mediocrity of my talents and pretenfions." It
was indeed in that of being private fecretary to
Lord Rockingham. But fince he fo humbly fpeaks
of his *mediocrity* of *talents*, *his little rank*, and his
no confequence, how comes it to pafs, that he thought
Mr. Cornwall addreffed himfelf to him ? He tells
you indeed, " it was only as well as his eyes could
" difcern it." From his own words you fhall derive the true reafon. " But a fituation near
" enough," fays he, " to fee as well as others
" what was going on." And hence it refults, as
men *muft* always *fee what is going on* in proportion to
their *powers* of *difcernment*, that he *pretends* to poffefs
an underftanding equal to the minifter himfelf, or
any of his coadjutors; or that the minifter faw things
according to the *mediocrity* of his fecretary's talents.
That the former was the *pretenfion* of your orator is
evident beyond difpute; for fays he, " I *did fee* in
" that noble perfon fuch found principles ; fuch
" an enlargement of mind ; fuch clear and faga-
" cious fenfe, and fuch an unfhaken fortitude, as
" have bound me, as well as others much better
" than me, by an invincible attachment to him
" from that forward." Thus you find, as he
could fee as well as others, what was going on,
and this minifter was *one* of the *things* which was
going on, he muft, logically, include all the great
qualities of his mafter ; or how could he have feen
things fo well as *he* did ? And hence you muft perceive that the *badnefs* of his *eyes*, being unable to
extend their views to the end of his vanity ; it was

by

by the influence of the latter that he appropriated Mr. Cornwall's addreſs to himſelf alone.

As to his *attachment* to the noble lord, I harbour no doubt, that it is as firm as that of the ivy to the wall, and for the ſame reaſon, that of being *ſupported*. You all know it is impoſſible for *one man* to determine what *another* ſees ; and therefore I can neither affirm nor deny, that Mr. Burke ſaw thoſe amazing qualities in the then firſt lord of the Treaſury. I ſhall take the liberty of hinting only, that as this orator *hears* what does *not* ſound to other *ears*, ſo he may ſee what is *inviſible* to the diſcernment of other mens *eyes*. I ſhall, however, examine the conduct of *that* miniſter as freely as *his* ſecretary has enquired into thoſe of other miniſters ; and then leave it to your determination, whether theſe ſuperlative qualities are become viſible to you.

I paſs the conduct of Lord Rockingham, reſpecting the Spaniſh trade of America, becauſe Mr. Burke " believes he ſoon ſaw his way in that " buſineſs." For he was his *guide, philoſopher,* and *friend*. And " the alarm which was taken by the " whole body in office, when his lordſhip began to " open his ground." Becauſe thoſe hoſtile preparations produced nothing to the preſent purpoſe. " The firſt ſtep the noble lord took, was to have " the opinion of his excellent, learned, and *ever-* " *lamented* friend the late Mr. York," more particularly as he deſerted him for the ſeals. " When his " lordſhip knew that formally and officially, which " in ſubſtance he had known before," from Mr. Burke, whoſe *maſculine underſtanding* had been *quickened* by the ſcience of the law, which makes *more* knaves than all the others upon earth. " He immediately diſpatched orders to " redreſs the grievance," reſpecting the Spaniſh trade.

trade. And Mr. Burke will fay,—— *willful* will do it. " For the then minifter, he is of that confti-
" tution of mind, that he knows he would have
" iffued, on the fame critical occafion, the very
" fame orders, if the acts of trade had been, as
" they were not, directly againſt him; and would
" have chearfully fubmitted to the equity of par-
" liament for his indemnity."

Now it appears to me, that this panegyriſt of Lord Rockingham, would have acted, to the full, as judiciouſly, if he had faid nothing of this no-ble lord's *conſtitution of mind*. Becauſe ſo prevalent a *difpofition* to act againſt law, on his *own* au-thority, does not feem to be the beſt adapted for being entruſted with the executive powers of a free ſtate. And I would willingly believe, that the fecretary has difcerned *no* fuch conftitution in his maſter. For it can never be a characteriſtic that will recommend him to his *fovereign*; or which ought to be eſteemed by you the *fubjects*. Be-fides this, his lordſhip does, I imagine, remember, that a king was once driven from the throne of this realm, for *difpenfing* with the *laws*; and that the *bill* of *rights* pronounces fuch acts *illegal*, even in a *fovereign*. Can a *minifter*, with prudence, therefore rely on the *indemnity* of parliament for fuch tranſgreſſions as have baniſhed kings? Befides this, does he not recollect, that an illuftrious an-ceſtor, than whom no mortal ever had a more illu-ſtrious, died on the ſcaffold, for fuch tranſactions as the laws could make *no crime*; although the blood-thirſty, and rebellious progenitors of thofe very fanatics, whofe unnatural caufe his lordſhip now ſupports, doomed him moſt murderouſly to death. Awake, my lord, awake, fly from your deluders; return to the glorious and the virtuous
principles

principles of the great earl of Stafford; your king, your country, your noble lineage, every laudable sensation of humanity invoke you to it. Shall a *Wentworth* join with the abettors of rebellion, and plead the cause of men descended from those who put his guiltless ancestor to death, and whose principles would now doom him to a like fate?

Your orator continues. "It was not till the "end of October that the news of the troubles, "on account of the stamp act, arrived in Eng- "land. No sooner had the sound of that mighty "tempest reached us in England, than the whole "of the then opposition, instead of feeling hum- "bled by the unhappy issue of their measures, "seemed to be infinitely elated, and cried out, "that the ministry, from envy to the glory of "their predecessors, were prepared to repeal the "stamp act."

As "this *seeming to be infinitely elated*, at the *unhappy* issue of their *own* measures; and that this *elation* should produce an outcry, that the ministry, from *envy* to the *glory* of their predecessors, were prepared to repeal the stamp act," appears to be extremely *unnatural*, I shall presume to assign another motive to this moral phænomenon. When this preceeding news arrived, the then opposition were not *elated* on the late *unhappy* issue of their *own* measures, but on that of the then ministry, who, when in opposition, by their harangues on the illegality of internally taxing the Americans, had filled their heads with falacious notions, and their hearts with the traiterous resolutions of resisting the legislative authority. The opposition saw the new ministry caught in their own toils, and instead of envying them the glory of the repeal, were *elated*; for such is the nature of man, that this mighty *tempest* had reached your shores, by
which

which they muſt be wrecked in the repeal of
the ſtamp act, caſt on ſhore and ſtripped of
power, place, intereſt, and eſteem. That the
event will juſtify this manner of thinking, cannot
be well called in queſtion. And this, I imagine,
will offer a better reaſon for this *joy* of oppoſition;
than the *unhappy* iſſue of their *own* meaſures;
for misfortunes are ſeldom accompanied with *plea-
ſure.*

Your orator perſiſts. " I do," ſays he, " put
" my hand upon my heart, and aſſure them, that
" they did *not* come to a reſolution directly to re-
" peal. They weighed this matter as its diffi-
" culty and importance required. They con-
" ſidered maturely among themſelves. They
" conſidered with all who could give advice or in-
" formation. It was not determined but a little
" before the meeting of parliament. But it was
" determined, and the main lines of their own
" plan marked out before that meeting. Two
" queſtions aroſe, (I hope I am not going into a
" narrative troubleſome to the houſe.). *

" [A cry of, go on, go on.]"

Oh, vanity, how ſtupendous is thy power on the
heart of man! This orator of *too ſcrupulous a delicacy*, inſerts in his printed ſpeech, that which he
imagines, was an oblation of applauſe at the altar
of his pre-eminence.

Before I proceed to a farther examination of the
conduct of the Rockingham miniſtry, it is abſolutely requiſite that I lay before you of what this
American tempeſt conſiſted. And that no intent
to

---

* Bathos. chap. 10. Apoſiopeſis.

to delude you by misreprefentation may be imputed to me, I will give it in your orator's own words. " The refolutions of the afiemblies were " violent ; the infurrections univerfal; the ftamp " papers were feized and burned ; the ftamp of- " ficers forced to refign their commiffions under " the gallows ; the houfes of the magiftrates were " rifled and pulled down ; they expelled from the " country all who dared to write or fpeak a fingle " word in defence of the powers of parliament.*

Such were the horrors that characterifed this American tempeft, and never were a captain and a crew fo aftonifhed and ftruck with terror, as the new minifter and his affociates, who had undertaken the conduct of the political fhip. They were all in the ftate of Scapin's mafter; each afking, *what the devil had he to do on fhip-board?*

Conviction came too late. They faw that their fpeeches, in oppofition to the parliamentary authority of taxing America, had produced not only a determined difobedience to the right of impofing *internal* but *external* taxes alfo; and they feared that nothing lefs than an abfolute renunciation of the legiflative authority of this realm over the colonies could calm this tempeft in America. This horrible apparition was accompanied with another not lefs terrifying ; a dread that the renouncing of the fovereign legiflative right would not only expofe them to utter deteftation and contempt in Britain, and in all the nations of the earth, but that fuch a pufillanimity of conduct muft fpeedily difmifs them from power and office, if they difregarded the late refolution of the commons, *firmly* and *effectually* to fupport his majefty.

to

---

* Speech, p. 71.

to fupprefs, thofe rebellious infurrections. At the
fame time, without yielding to the demands,
which they, in their harangues, had fo ftrenuoufly
pronounced to be the rights of the colonies, they
knew not how to extricate themfelves from their
embarrafsments on that fide. Thus, like rats,
feduced, by the love of bacon, into a wire-trap,
the new miniftry found themfelves unable to get
out, or to ftay *in* with fafety. No terms can more
aptly exprefs their terrible perplexity, than thofe
which your orator hath offered in their juftification.

"The firft of the two confiderations, fays he,
" was whether the repeal fhould be total, or
" whether only partial, taking out every thing
" burthenfome and productive, and referving only
" an empty acknowledgement, fuch as a *ftamp* on
" cards or dice." Hence it appears, that the firft
confideration of thofe new ftatefmen, who had oppofed the *ftamp-act* as illegal, was to *prove*, they
had acted *againft* their *confciences*, by keeping a
ftamp-act ftill exifting. But this they foon perceived would not fucceed. Confcience had no bufinefs to interfere in that affair. Thus their own
profeffions, purfuits, and pretended principles,
that the parliament had no right to tax America,
being unreprefented, ferved them as the wires
ferved the rats. They had let them in, but on attempting to get out, they ran in their faces, and
made them too fore for further attempts of efcaping that way. For this *empty* acknowledgement
of a parliamentary right to lay a ftamp duty on cards
or dice, like the orator's *empty recital*, would have
been brimful of ruin to their continuance in the
miniftry. As all mankind would have then feen their
abandoned conduct; in having oppofed that very

L   right

right and that very tax which they would now exert and continue exactly in the fame manner which they condemned. Such a tranfaction would have rendered them not only detefted as men void of principle; but ridiculous as divefted of common underftanding. Yet even that intention, fo demonftrative of their injuftice, in oppofing Mr. Grenville; fo replete with the exhibition of their own folly by its having been once in meditation; and fo needlefs to be revealed at prefent, hath the wifdom of your refponfible orator laid before the commons in *founds*, and your in *print*! Is it not probable that, from a perfuafion, that fuch *derogating difcoveries* would proceed from his attempting to *juftify* himfelf and his mafter, that the cry of *go on, go on*, arofe, which he attributes to the *approbation* of his auditors.

"The other queftion, he adds, was on what " principle the act fhould be repealed." Hence it is clear, that thefe minifters, when in oppofition, had oppofed this act on *no principle*. For had they acted on *principle*, that on which it was *oppofed* would have *equally* ferved for its being *repealed*. However, "on the head of this principle two " principles were ftarted." This ftarting of *two* principles upon the *head* of *one* principle is a happy imitation of his favourite authority.* One of thefe was, "that the legiflative rights of this " country, with regard to America, were not " entire, but had certain reftrictions and limitati- " ons." This, although it were the chief argument on which, in oppofition, they had exploded the parliamentary right of taxing America, they were withheld from carrying into execution. And does

* Bathos. chap. 10. Of the variegating, confounding, and reverfing figures.

does not that circumstance fully evince that their former arguments, and their consciences had been constantly at war; or that their fortitude was unequal to the demands to which those declarations had reduced them ? This discovery shews you also that your orator is undesignedly battering the place he would defend.

" The other principle was, that taxes of this
" kind were contrary to the fundamental princi-
" ples of commerce, on which the colonies were
" founded ; and contrary to every idea of poli-
" tical equity ; by which equity we are bound as
" much as possible to extend the spirit and benefit
" of the British constitution to every part of the
" British dominions." But on what ground is this principle supported ? is the peremptory averment of this orator sufficient to obtain it credit ? the experience of all ages contradicts this opinion. For, in what state, either ancient or modern, founded on commercial principles, was there no internal taxation ? was such the case at Tyre, Carthage, Athens, or any other commercial realm of antiquity ? is it so, at this day, in Venice, Genoa, or Holland ?

The constitution of England indeed was not founded on commercial principles. Yet so much of these principles hath been woven into its original fabric since its commencement, that it may, not improperly, be deemed a commercial govern- ment. And such is the fact, that *internal taxes* have been multiplied with the *augmentation* of her *trade*. That trade alone hath supplied the means of payment. And by that trade the nation hath been amazingly enriched. This being the spi- rit of the British constitution; whence does it arise that it is contrary to every idea of *political equity*, to proceed in a similar mode in America? as

L 2

this

this speaker affirms, "we are bound, as much as possible, by that *equity*, to extend the *spirit* and the *benefit* of the British constitution to every part of the British dominions." And thus, in compliance with his own precepts, he and his minister *extended* the spirit of the British constitution into America, by *abrogating* a law which was made in conformity to the undeviating practice of that very *constitution?*

He continues, "the option both of the measure,
" and of the principle of the repeal was made be-
" fore the session; and I wonder, says he, how
" any one can read the king's speech, at the open-
" ing of that session, without seeing in that speech,
" both the repeal and the declaratory act very suf-
" ficiently crayoned out. Those who cannot
" see this can see nothing." It was under
that *ministry alone*, that in the speech from
the throne, the parliament hath been informed what
laws they were to repeal, and what to support.
Was it not an *invasion* on the rights of the subjects by which those ministers were guilty of high
crimes and misdemeanour? and yet it is avowed by
Edmund Burke, *then clerk* to lord Rockingham,
who *now* presents himself, in this defence, as
the chief and *responsible minister* of *state*. But
as these two acts were only *crayoned* out in sketches,
and probably by *himself*, it so happened that the
usual unintelligibility of his designs accompanied
them. And thus the meaning of them was for-
tunately concealed from all but *himself* and his *dis-
ciples.*

" A partial repeal," says he, "or as the *bon ton*
" of the court then was, a *modification*, would
" have satisfied a timid, unsystematic, procrasti-
" nating ministry, as such a measure has since done
                                        " such

" such a miniftry." It feems probable that an affertion fo confident, till that moment, had never been
uttered in the face of men, who ftood convinced that
the fhort duration of that feeble miniftry confifted
folely of timidity, want of fyftem, and procraftina-
tion. This you fhall fee indifputably evinced. And
then the comparifon of their conduct, and that of the
prefent miniftry fhall falfify the latter affertion, and
prove that "the very modification which is the con-
" ftant refource of weak undeceiving minds," was
that which attended the Rockingham adminiftration in this affair.

"To repeal," fays he, "by a denial of our
" right to tax, in the preamble (and this too did
" not want advifers) would have cut, in the he-
" roic ftile, the Gordion knot with a fword." A
fword compofed of a majority of votes in the
houfe of commons. "Either meafure, he con-
" tinues, would have coft no more than a day's
" debate." What an execrable idea of the fovereign legiflative authority of this kingdom does
that audacious affertion impart. The *king*, the
lords, the *commons* would have refcinded the lawful
power of the realm; and the rights of the people;
and have abfolutely fubverted this conftitution,
had lord Rockingham thought it proper. It is an
affertion fuch as hath never been pronounced by
the lips of any man, antecedent to this fpeech.
It is an affertion fo replete with indignity to the
peers, and your *reprefentatives*, that nothing but a
fettled contempt for him that fpoke it, could have
permitted its paffing with impunity. It is an imputation of abandoned profligacy, carried up even
to the *throne* itfelf; when at no time, fince the fun
hath rifen on this kingdom. did the diadem fur-
round the head of any fovereign who lefs deferved

fo

fo impious an outrage on his character. His fteadi-
nefs and zeal to fuftain the legiflative authority
through all his dominions, even when the Americans are taking arms to place his prerogative
fuperior to that power, pronounce the preceding
paffage, of this orator, to be a calumny unprecedented in the hiftory of the world, and in the malevolence of man.

He perfifts. " But when the total repeal was
" adopted ; and adopted on principles of po-
" licy, of equity, and of commerce ; this plan
" made it neceffary to enter into many and diffi-
" cult meafures." Of their principles of policy,
equity, and commerce, I have already fpoken.
It fhall foon be confirmed by their own conduct in getting out of their difficulties, of what
they confifted. And now I will regale you with
a paffage, that excels, in the Babylonifh jargon of
unintelligible metaphor, all that has hitherto appeared, either in fpeech or writing.

" It became neceffary," fays he, " to open a
" very large *field* of *evidence*, *commenfurate to* thefe
" extenfive *views* ; but then this *labour* did *knights*
" *fervice*. It opened the *eyes* of feveral to the
" true ftate of the American affairs : it *enlarged*
" their *ideas* ; it *removed prejudices* ; and it *concilia-*
" *ted* the *opinions* and *affections* of men." This
figure, fo replete with impracticable and incongruous imagery, is taken from his idea of the old
feudal government of this realm. The *villains*, or
flaves, whofe bufinefs it was to drudge in huf-
bandry, *opened* a very large *field*. You have heard
of *a field* of *corn*, *a field* of *hay*, *a field* of *pafture*, and
a field of *battle* ; but when was a *field* of *evidence* ever
opened before the 19*th April*, 1774. This *field*,
however, fo *neceffary* for *evidence*, was not for the
at-

attainment of *truth* and *knowledge* from the testimonies to be brought before the parliament. It was to give the ministry a *fine prospect*, commensurate to their *extensive views*, which seems to be an odd bußnefs for *evidence*. But then this *labour* of *slaves* and *villains*, did *knights fervice*. And thus their *bedging* and *ditching*, and *opening of fields*, was the *fervice* of *freemen* ; the *attending* of their *sovereign* and their *lords in arms*, and at their *courts?* This being so ftrange an innovation, one would imagine it might have fufficed for any man. But a genius of fuch magnitude as is your orator, is not to be contented with being *his own parallel*, he will *excel himfelf*. And therefore this *villains knights fervice*, did not confift in *opening* of fields, nor in *bearing* arms, but in *opening* of *eyes*; and thus it did the fervice of an *oculift*. It ftopped not there. It *enlarged ideas*, and thus it did the fervice of *learning*. It removed *prejudices*, and thus it did the fervice of *philofophy*. It *conciliated* mens *opinions*, and thereby ferved as a *peace-maker*. Hence it appears that the minifter was a *villain*, a *knight*, an *oculift*, a *preceptor*, a *philofopher*, and a *juftice* of the *peace*, all at one time, and on the fame bußnefs. With what luxuriant exhibition of the *profund*, are your minds regaled ! * Imitated from thofe paffages, where the Almighty is reprefented as a *mercer*, a *baker*, a *butler*, a *goldbeater*, a *fuller*, &c. But the preceding profundities in the bathos were felected from a variety of paffages in feveral books. In this unparalleled fpeech of this celebrated author, they ftand like foldiers in a line, with each a *different uniform*.

L 4   It

---

* Ch. 5. of the true genius for the profund, and by what it is conftituted.

It would, however, be a flagrant injuſtice to deny, that the nimbleneſs of his imagination, in leaping from one object to another, is prodigious. The great Socrates is repreſented as,being an admirer of agility, and to meaſure the leaps of that wonder of agility a flea. I would therefore hope, that this *great* orator will not be offended at my comparing his *nimble* fancy with that minute exiſtence. I confeſs, however, the *former never ſtings.* They both leap from ſpot to ſpot, in ſuch directions as expreſs no intent of proceeding to any particular end. They are inviſible in their paſſage from place to place. At every pauſe you are conſtantly ſurprized to ſee them, where they were never expected: until at length they both diſappear, by ſpringing, the Lord knows whither.

Such being the numerous employments in which the miniſter was then engaged. He tells you, " the noble Lord Rockingham, who then took " the *lead in* adminiſtration." Your orator ſtill going *before* him, like the mace-bearer preceding the ſpeaker of the Commons, to expreſs his dignity and direct the way. " His honoured friend " under him, Mr. Dowdeſwell; and a right hon. " gentleman, general Conway (if he will not re- " ject his ſhare, and it was a large one in his " buſineſs) exerted the moſt laudable indu- " ſtry, in bringing before the houſe the fulleſt, " moſt important, and leaſt *garbled body* of evi- " dence that were ever produced to that houſe." To *garble* a *parcel* of evidence, may be allowable in figure ; but the *brokers* declare, a *body* is *not* to be *garbled,* either in *fact* or *figure.*

He now tells you, " the enquiry," which included all the preceding ſervices, " laſted in the " com-

" committee for fix weeks; and at its conclusion
" this houfe, by an independent, noble, fpirited,
" and unexpected majority ; by a majority that
" will redeem all the acts ever done by majorities
" in parliament." Will it redeem the riot act,
the feptennial act, the acts that have mortgaged
your anceftors and yourfelves, and will continue the
fame burthen on your pofterity for the payment
of the intereft of thofe millions which were raifed
in fupport of Dutchmen and Germans in former
wars, and of the Americans in the laft? If the
mifchief of all thefe, and a number of other acts
be redeemed, by repealing this ftamp act, on what
account do the miniftry proceed, as if thefe ftatutes
were ftill in full energy? why do you pay thefe
taxes, which are *redeemed* by parliament? why is
the minifter unimpeached that ftill dares to collect
them? Otherwife is it not a *redemption*, where *nothing* is *redeemed*? An impofition on your underftandings attempted by this orator, who thus prefumes to treat you as an undifcerning populace?
But whence did this fudden transformation arife,
of being independent, noble, and fpirited in
this majority, who you are told, in this very page,
of his oration, were ready to have *denied* the Britifh
right of taxing the Americans? This readinefs,
and that which would have been the effect of its
being employed, may probably be deemed, an act
of a noble and fpirited majority, by this orator.
But were there no *dependent* members who contri-
buted to that majority? Could it have been *unexpected*, by *him*, when he has already declared,
they were *fure* that it would have coft but a day's
debate to renounce the Britifh authority over America? He is eternally combating his own affertions,

tions, like a cock that fights with his own image in a glafs, unknowing that it is himfelf. Could but this propitiatory act of redemption, extend its influence to the other world, what a multitude of members would then afcend from the depths of Erebus, to dwell in the celeftial manfions!

" However, this act of redemption was accom-
" plifhed in the teeth of all the old mercenary
" Swifs of ftate ; in defpite of all the fpeculators
" and augurs of political events ; in defiance of
" the whole embattled legion of veteran penfi-
" oners, and practifed inftruments of court, gave
" a total repeal to the ftamp act ; and (if it had
" been fo permitted) a lafting peace to this
" whole empire." It will be no e: 'y tafk to dif-
cover a paffage *more* replete with the fpirit of malignancy, and with *lefs* of the fpirit of truth and fatire. His arrows are altogether pointlefs, and even his bolts do not bruife, although they be foon fhot. The whole is a venomous parody of that language, which is fo fuccefsfully practifed by the ladies, who, for their amufement, traffic in fifh. By the Swifs of ftate, I imagine he means ftate Swifs. And on this occafion, the *old* and mercenary were fupplied by the *new* and merce-nary, who oppofed *their* teeth to *thofe* of the *others*; few of whom did not pafs into the fame fervice under the new leader. Even the defpite of fpeculators and augurs in political events, was op-pofed by a like motive in like men ; and a *new* legion of *new* penfioners, in which moft of the *old* inlifted, was embattled on this occafion of repeal-ing the ftamp act. For by what other than mer-cenary means, was a majority obtained in all that parliament ? It is true indeed, that the repeal of the ftamp act would have given as lafting a peace

to

the empire of this kingdom over America, as fe-
vering the head of Charles the firſt with an axe, did
to his ſovereignty over this kingdom. But in political diſeaſes, death is ſometimes but apparent,
and there the means of recovering ſubſiſts. Such
was happily the caſe in this inſtance.

" I ſtate," ſays your orator, " theſe particulars,
" becauſe this act of ſpirit and fortitude, has lately
" been, in the circulation of the ſeaſon, and in
" ſome hazarded declamations in this houſe, attri-
" buted to timidity. If the conduct of miniſtry,
" in propoſing the repeal, had ariſen from timi-
" dity, with regard to themſelves, it would have
" been greatly to be condemned. Intereſted ti-
" midity diſgraces as much in the cabinet, as per-
" ſonal timidity does in the field. But timidity,
" with regard to the well-being of our country,
" is heroic virtue." By the *circulation* of the ſeaſon, for ſurely no ſeaſon *circulates*, I imagine he
means the *progreſſion* of it. It is his *preſcriptive*
right, in *words*, to bend the inflexible ſtraight lines
of nature into circles, but never to make the
crooked paths ſtraight. I will examine this idea
of timidity, which your orator has delivered. "Intereſted timidity he allows, diſgraces as much in
the cabinet, as perſonal timidity does in the field ;
but *timidity*, with regard to the *well-being* of our
country, is *heroic virtue.*" Hence it follow, that
the miniſter, who *trembles* with *fear*, when the *well-
being* of his *country* calls him forth to arduous action, is a *man* both *virtuous* and *heroic*. Is it not
an opinion, hitherto unavowed, that timidity, reſpecting the welfare of your country, is virtuous,
which it is the indiſpenſible duty of every ſubject
to promote and to defend, a welfare which exceeds that of perſon in degree, as millions are
more

more in number than an individual ; a welfare which can never be deserted by a minister but through a flagitious infensibility of honour ; a renunciation of every claim to fortitude ; a dereliction of his duty to exert that executive power with which he is entrusted ! all which disgrace the very being of humanity : and yet a timidity which includes all these your orator hath dared to dignify with the name of *heroic virtue.*

On this opinion of heroic and virtuous timidity, so irreconcileable with every conception of magnanimity, it was, that this secretary and his master founded their conduct, respecting the welfare of your country in repealing the stamp act. And this he verifies, by avowing, " the noble lord who " then conducted affairs, and his worthy colleagues, " whilst they *trembled* at the prospect of such di- " stresses as the Commons and ministry have since " brought upon themselves, were not *afraid* stea- " dily to look in the face that glaring and dazzling " influence, at which the eyes of eagles have " blenched."

I will first examine the state of affairs in America, in order to explain whether the *trembling* of this noble lord and his colleagues, so perfectly *worthy* of being conjoined with him, and which produced the repeal of the stamp act, be an *heroic* virtue. And then I will examine that fortitude, " with which they looked in the face, that dazzling influence at which the eyes of eagles have *blenched.*" To this intent, I shall select the words of this speaker, as those which can best protect me from the charges of prejudice and partiality, in describing the conduct of the Americans at that time. You have already heard from *him,* " that *insurrections* were *universal* ; the *stamp papers seized*
and

and *burned* ; the *officers forced* to *refign* their commiffions under the *gallows* ; the *houfes* of the *magiftrates rifled* and *pulled down*, and all who dared
to *write* and *fpeak* in defence of the powers of
parliament, *expelled* their *country*."

To thefe he adds, " when the accounts of the
" American governors came before the houfe,
" they appeared ftronger even than the warmth
" of public imagination had painted them.——
" All the late difturbances, which have been,
" at one time, the minifters motives for the re-
" peal of five out of fix of the new court taxes ;
" and are now the pretence for refufing to repeal
" the fixth, did not amount to——Why do I
" compare them ? No, not a tenth part of the
" tumults and violence which prevailed long be-
" fore the repeal of that act.*

The intent to remove Mr. Grenville from adminiftration, together with the others who held
the fuperior offices, took its rife from the injudicious omiffion of the princefs of Wales, in the act
for eftablifhing a regency. As this event was
fudden, the fupplying of their places was attended
with fome precipitation. The marquis of Rockingham, as it was then faid and believed, was reluc-
tantly induced to accept the lead in the Treafury
and in adminiftration. The veteran duke of New-
caftle, in the place of privy-feal, was appointed
dry-nurfe ; and Edmund Burke, in the name of
private fecretary, was made rocker to the young
minifter.

As forefight is not one of the attributes with
which your orator has fo fplendidly adorned his
minifter, the approach of the ftorm from America
was

* P. 69. of the fpeech.

was not difcerned. Accordingly, when it was known in this kingdom, the new minifters began to perceive, that their preceding conduct in parliament, had produced much greater difturbance than they expected or defired; now the executive power of the ftate was fallen into their own hands. In confequence of this event, they became as uneafy as rats in a hot kettle, and as unacquainted by what means to efcape from their fcalding fituation.

Their embarrafsments were as great as they were unforefeen. On the part of this kingdom, the fovereign authority ftared them full in the face, and demanded to be fuftained. On the part of the colonies, thofe principles and opinions which thefe minifters, when in oppofition, had avowed in parliament; and which had incenfed the Americans to thofe outrages in which they were then engaged, called on them to renounce the parliamentary right, not only of internal, but of all taxation, becaufe the colonifts were not reprefented in the houfe of commons. Such was the fituation of affairs in England, when the Rockingham miniftry afcended to power.

As the Americans had extended their objections to *external* equally with *internal* taxation, that circumftance would have afforded the new miniftry a favorable opportunity of difentangling themfelves from the briars in which they were caught. But it paffed unobferved by all the great faculties of the minifter and his worthy collegues. It was evident that by thefe men the repeal of the ftamp-act could not be refufed, becaufe it was an *internal* tax, which they had uniformly decried. But the right to *external* taxation fhould have been fupported becaufe they themfelves, in oppofition, had allowed it to be conftitutional. At the fame time, to annihilate all caufe of contention, refpecting the right of
parliament

parliament over the Americans, that miniftry fhould
have propofed to them the fending of members to
the houfe of commons.

This conduct would have perfectly coincided
with their former profeffions and pretexts, in adopt-
ing the caufe of the Americans. It would have
imparted the face of principle and defign in their
oppofition to the preceding miniftry. Had the colonies acquiefced in this propofition of reprefentatives, the grand object of preferving the legiflative authority over America had been obtained,
and the caufe of clamour in America removed.
If the colonifts had refufed to comply with that propofal, that obftinacy would have evinced their intentions of detaching themfelves from all parliamentary influence ; have juftified the proceedings
of the minifter to fuftain the fupreme authority of
Britain ; and have produced one univerfal refentment of their impudence and injuftice in this country. As either one or other of thefe events muft
have been the confequence of the preceding conduct, it is manifeft they were then fo aufpicioufly cir-
cumftanced as to poffefs the means of efcaping from
their dreaded difficulties with reputation. But the
found principles, the *enlarged mind*, the *fagacious fenfe*
and the *unfhaken fortitude* which Mr. Burke faw
in his matter conducted him by another road, the
effects of which fhall foon be laid before you.

With a view to obviate the charge of facrificing
the Britifh fovereignty to the rebellion of the colonifts, the minifters paffed an act declaratory of
the legiflative right to tax America without *qualification* refpecting either the *external* or *internal*
mode of laying duties, and then by another they
repealed the ftamp-act *totally*.*

By.

---

* Speech, p. 66.

By the firſt they imagined that every imputation of having ſurrendered the legiſlative authority to the inſolence of the coloniſts, would be moſt effectually averted. If the immenſe talents of that miniſter be to be decided by this procedure, it evinces he was a novice in the ſcience of human kind. For, inſtead of effecting what they expected, it proved to demonſtration, their *unprincipled* proceedings in oppoſition to the late miniſtry; ſince it contradicted all that they had avowed reſpecting the *limited* right of parliament to tax America *unrepreſented*. It confirmed the opinion that the previous adminiſtration had acted juſtly and conſtitutionally in obtaining the ſtamp-act; and that the *then* miniſtry had oppoſed them with a conſciouſneſs of *their* being wrong in that oppoſition. And thus they ſtood as ſelf condemned and deſpicable culprits, ratified by their own act in parliament.

By this *unqualified* act of the legiſlature alſo, the Americans were in fact made rebels againſt the ſovereign authority. For the parliamentary right of enacting the ſtamp-act being now legiſlatively declared to be conſtitutional, the outrages which had been committed in the colonies were conſequently determined to be rebellious. This was the firſt ſervice the new miniſters performed for their American favourites, whoſe cauſe they had eſpouſed. Thus, as the reſult of his own proceedings, as well as by the duty of his office, it became an indiſpenſible obligation on the new miniſter to compel the Americans to an acknowledgement of the Britiſh right of legiſlature, before the ſtamp-act was repealed; or never to have repealed it. On the contrary, without exerting the leaſt endeavour to obtain the ſlighteſt conceſſion from the coloniſts, that the parliamentary authority was legally exerciſed in

America,

America, they repealed the ftamp-act *totally*, and without conditions. And yet by this conduct, did that miniftry expect to continue in the enjoyment of power, place, and riches, approved both by Britons and Americans.

But fo diffimilar was the event to the expectation; that the people of England beheld this declaratory and *unqualified* act, like the waxen figure of king William, in a glafs cafe, in Weftminfter-Abbey, decorated with all the trappings and infignia of fovereignty, the ineffective mockery of life and power; a delufion by which their underftandings were to be infulted. And thus by the minifterial affectation of afcertaining the parliamentary right by law, and renouncing it in practice by the repeal of the ftamp-act, the people were led to confider that repeal, as an act declaratory that they intended virtually to abolifh the Britifh fovereignty in America, which they had fpecioufly fupported by parliament. Hence a conviction naturally enfued, that the then miniftry were regardlefs of their country's honour; funk in abject timidity; and attentive folely to their own interefts.

On the other hand, the Americans beheld this declaratory and *unqualified* act, fometimes as a fcandalous defertion of thofe principles and arguments which thefe minifters, when in oppofition, had fo unrefervedly avowed and promifed to fupport. At others they confidered it as totally void of all principle, as they had now attempted to eftablifh an authority which they had conftantly averred the parliament did not legally poffefs: and therefore, intending to fix that power which they could not juftify, they were refolved to exceed the former, and to act more arbitrarily in their adminiftration. At the fame time they

M

ab-

abstained not from deriding the new ministerial idea of establishing a parliamentary right,
over America, by that very *parliament* whose authority, these ministers had formerly sustained, and
taught them to believe, was inadequate to that
right. The repeal of the stamp-act was therefore
received as a temporary expedient to reduce *them*
to tranquility, whilst the ministerial intrigues were
carrying on for permanently fixing the legislative
authority in the colonies. By these proceedings,
nothing was settled but discontent both in Britain
and America,

In this behaviour, the discerning saw no mark
either of a sound principle, an enlarged mind, a
sagacious sense, or an unshaken fortitude. But they
beheld a rich redundance of the *heroic virtue* of
being absolutely *intimidated* from acting with regard
to the *welfare* of their *country.* They saw them
virtuously sculking behind a *majority* in parliament
in this kingdom ; and *heroically fleeing* before the
rebels in America, with that contempt for their
understandings, and indignation at their pusilla-
nimity which they deserved.

The whole of this singular transaction was conducted by the self-interested and despicable cunning
of a cheesemonger, chosen arbitrator between his
two customers, Tom Thimble the taylor, and
Ebenezar Slipthumb the woollen-draper. Matthew Maggot, " *because a modification is the constant*
" *resource of weak and undeciding minds,*" resolved
to *refine* and to preserve His *interest* with both parties. By this policy, he doubted not but still to
continue in the emoluments arising from the sale
of his old Cheshire and double Gloucester.
With vast circumspection, and self-applause, he
therefore determined, that Tom *had* the *right* to
what

what he demanded ; but that Ebenezar should be excused *from* complying *with it*. Tom was displeased, becaufe he thought a right which was not to be exerted, was of no value. Ebenezar, becaufe the right was againft him, and altho' it were not now to be exerted, it might be on future occasions. And thus by this refinement in *clear* and *sagacious fenfe, Matthew* loft both his cuftomers ; fell into difgrace among his neighbours, refpecting his intellects and felfifhnefs; was deferted by his former followers ; became a fufferer in his profits ; and a bankrupt in reputation.

Such was the conduct of that miniftry, who were not to be fatisfied with " the *bon ton* of the " court, a *modification* like the prefent timid, un- " fyftematic, procraftinating miniftry, becaufe a " modification is the conftant refource of weak " undeciding minds." This reflection undoubtedly comes with double *propriety* and *juftnefs* from your orator, and his mafter, who through *timidity* fled before the Americans in rebellion. Who were *fyftematically* wrong, by enacting one law and repealing another. Who difpleafed both fides of the queftion, and hoped to *procraftinate* the evil day of an open rupture, and their own difmiffion, Whereas the prefent miniftry are, and have been with real fortitude *fyftematically* advancing to fubdue that rebellion, which was excited by this orator and his worthy affociates.

Such having been their exhibition of the *heroic virtue* of *timidity*, relative to the Americans, I come now to fhew the unfhaken fortitude of the noble lord and his worthy colleagues, "who were not afraid to look in the face that glaring and dazzling influence at which the eyes of eagles have blenched." And what do you imagine

this

this *dazzling influence* was, at which the *more* than *eagle-eyed ministry* did *not* blench? it was " the *face* " of one of the ablest, and let him fay, not the " moft fcrupulous oppofitions that ever was in that " houfe, and withftood it, unaided even by one " of the ufual fupports of adminiftration." Oh what an act of heroifm was here. Let no man henceforth mention Leonidas, againft the Perfians, at the ftraits of Thermopylæ!

By being unfupported by *one* of the ufual *fupports*, I imagine he muft mean that *one* called a *found judgement*. For is there a man fo ignorant or fo credulous as to believe they were not backed by all thofe other fupports of power, place, and money, that obtained all other majorities? How unfhaken in more than eagle-eyed fortitude was this minifter? he looked *unblenching* in the face of oppofition, againft which had he been accompanied with two hundred and eighty dwarfs in underftanding, ftrength and courage, provided they poffeffed the dangerlefs intrepidity of faying *Aye*, he muft inevitably have overcome two hundred and feventy eight opponents, although each of them had been a giant in all the preceding faculties of foul and body. An act fo fingularly heroic, that none but an orator fo fingularly poffeffed of all the powers of rhetoric, could have executed the tafk of being his adequate panegyrift. An orator, who more than *eagle-eyed* fo glorioufly fought with his colleagues in this dazzling battle; after they had fled from rebels to their country, without daring to offer the leaft oppofition. And this, *like* Demofthenes in running away only, he would perfuade you was a deed of unfhaken fortitude.

But of what action will he leave the juftification unattempted, who fays that the minifter in this

conqueft

conqueſt in the houſe of commons, "was unaided
by even *one of the uſual ſupports of adminiſtration.*"

Not a man of the treaſury, admiralty, trade,
and plantation boards, not a placeman, penſioner,
nor officer civil or military, voted in the repeal of
this bill ; none but diſintereſted and independent
members. This he had the confidence to ſpeak in
the face of hundreds, conſcious, both *he* and *they,*
that it was untrue. This he has the confidence to
publiſh to you who are in like manner convinced
of this untruth. This too I ſuppoſe he will deem
an act of unſhaken fortitude. It is indeed an act
that may juſtly create aſtoniſhment, at leaſt, in
any man except this orator.

But the fortitude of the miniſter was exerciſed
in a yet more courageous manner. " He looked
" in the face a perſon he had long re'pected and re-
" garded, and whoſe *aid* was then particularly want-
" ed: he means lord Chatham. He did this when
" he paſſed the declaratory act." From this paſſage,
it is evident that this ſpeaker conſiders the lord,
juſt mentioned, as a more formidable opponent
than all the oppoſition of the other commons.
But whence did it ariſe that this miniſter of ſuch
enlargement of mind, ſuch clear and ſagacious
ſenſe, ſhould want the aſſiſtance of that lord?
was the looking him in the face an act of unſhaken
fortitude, when he had no other way to look?
and yet you ſhall find, from the words of this very
ſpeaker, that no man could in fact be leſs formidable, than this lord ; if his pourtraiture of him
be juſt.

" It is now given out," ſays your orator, " for
" the uſual purpoſes, that lord Rockingham did
" not conſent to the repeal of the ſtamp act, un-
" til he was bullied into it by lord Chatham ;

M 3   ".and

" and the reporters have gone fo far, as publicly
" to affert, in an hundred companies, that ge-
" neral Conway, who propofed the repeal in the
" American committee, had another fet of re-
" folutions in his pocket, directly the reverfe of
" thofe he moved.   Thefe artifices of a defperate
" caufe are, at this time, fpread abroad with in-
" credible care, as if the induftry of the circula-
" tion were to make amends for the abfurdity of
" of the report."   And then, as a refutation of
this abfurdity, he fays, " whether the noble lord
" is of a complexion to be bullied by lord Chat-
" ham, or by any man, I muft fubmit to thofe who
" know him," with which I acquiefce.   And thus
this charge of timidity, fo abfurd and fo induftrioufly
propagated in converfation, is now *propagated* in
print, and left without a refutation ; and you hear
no more of the fecond fet of refolutions in general
Conway's pocket.   Does not this evafion of anfwer appear to be adopted, becaufe the affertions
cannot be difproved ?

It is pleafant to fee, with what aggravation of
magnanimity, this fpeaker reprefents lord Rockingham on this occafion.   " I confefs, when I
" look back to that time," fays he, " I confider
" him as placed in one of the moft trying fituati-
" ons in which, perhaps, any man ever ftood ? in
" the houfe of peers, there were very few of the
" miniftry, out of the noble lord's particular con-
" nexion, (except lord Egmont, who acted, as
" far as he could difcern, an honourable part) that
" did not look to fome other future arrangement,
" which warped his politics."   This trying fituation I have already explained, and he informs you,*
left

* Speech, p. 65.

left you should believe him, "they had powerful
"friends, the means of fighting a great battle, and
"of gaining the victory," which was certainly *as trying a situation as ever man did stand in.* But these
lords, whose honour he presumes so egregiously to
traduce, did nevertheless vote with the noble lord.
They did indeed, as he says, look to some future
arrangement, which *did not warp their politics,*
but confirmed their judgement, that the noble
lord's time of administration was expiring. "There
"were, in truth, in both houses, new and me-
"nacing appearances that might very naturally
"drive any other than a most resolute minister
"from his measure, or from his station." I have
already spoken sufficiently of his *resolution.* His
measure he was permitted to carry to his ruin as
a minister ; for in consequence of that measure, he
soon lost his station. "The houshold troops
"openly revolted ; the allies of the ministry (who
"refused responsibility for any) endeavoured to
"undermine their credit, and took ground that
"must be fatal to the success of the very cause
"which they would be thought to countenance."
In what a pitiful state of desertion does he place
that minister, whom he intends to laud and mag-
nify; and to whom he is indebted for the means
of all that importance which he so superciliously
assumes. Is it not a judicious method of supporting the character he was delineating for posterity,
to represent both houses of parliament surveying
him as a man, who by statute declaring the right
of parliament to tax the Americans, first makes
them rebels; and then by another, dismisses them
unacknowledging the offence, with the gratification
of their demands ? Who deserts the executive
power of the state, and offers up the supreme au-

M 4   thority

thority of the realm to timidity, and the groundlefs expectation of preferving his poft, which they
faw to be impoffible. Sir John Falftaffe values
himfelf for his knowing the true prince by the inftinct of a lion. Both houfes difcovered the minifter
by a very different kind of inftinct. It was that of
rats, which always defert a falling houfe.

"The queftion of the repeal was brought on by
" miniftry, in the very inftant when it was known
" that more than one court negociation was carry-
" ing on with the heads of the oppofition." And
at that inftant it was too late for the minifter to re-
cede. "Every thing, on every fide, was full of
" traps and mines," and thofe for whom they
were intended, were either caught in the former,
or were blown up by the latter. But it was not
the two houfes, and the court alone, which
difcerned the mifchief he was bringing on his
country. "Earth below fhook; heaven above
" menaced, all the elements of minifterial fafety
" were diffolved." But to what intent was all this
convulfion? It was, that earth expreffed her
difapprobation of his proceeding; the heavens
menaced him with their wrath; and what is more
than all, *indiffoluble* things, even *elements*, were *diffolved:* and thus he ftood periloufly difapproved
by heaven, earth, and man. I confefs indeed that
this is the firft time I ever heard that heaven and
earth, or any thing elfe, could be *elements* of minifterial fafety. Does he mean by thefe *elements*,
that there was *no* more *money* in the *Treafury*, and
that therefore they were diffolved?

"It was in the midft of this *chaos* of plots and
counterplots," heaven, earth, and man, plotting
and counterplotting againft a minifter, whom they
faw to need no other plots nor counterplots than
                                                    his

his own *found principle, enlarged mind, fagacious
fenfe, and unfhaken fortitude,* affifted by thofe of his
fecretary, to bring upon him inevitable ruin.
However, " it was in the midft of this complicated
" warfare, againft public oppofition and private
" treachery, that the firmnefs of that noble per-
" fon was put to the proof. He never ftirred from
" his ground ; no, not an inch." He was fure of
a majority in this repeal : on the accomplifhment of
which the general defertion of all around him took
place. And with refpect to his firmnefs, *of not
ftirring an inch,* it is evident, he had *not* an inch
to ftir; unlefs he had practifed that heroic timidity
of yielding before the oppofition, without one ver-
bal conteft, as he did before the rebellious Americans. " He remained fixed and determined in
" principle, in meafure, and in conduct." How
fatal thefe have proved to this country, has been
already fhewn, and fhall be farther elucidated.
" He practifed no managements." Is it not manifeft, that he knew nothing of management ?
" He fecured no retreat." There was no man
oppofed his going off. " He fought no apolo-
" gy." He left that to his fecretary, and it is
executed as the caufe deferves.
" I will likewife do juftice," he adds, " I ought
" to do it, to general Conway ; far from the du-
" plicity, wickedly charged on him, he acted his
" part with alacrity and refolution." Whether
he acted with duplicity or not, I have neither
grounds on which to determine, nor inclination to
charge him with fuch behaviour. But of this I am
fure, I fhould requeft every friend, who intended
to be my advocate againft double-dealing, to ufe
better arguments in difproof of it, " than acting
with alacrity and refolution." For thefe are as
equally

equally reconcilable with duplicity as with the moft
fimple deed that can be tranfacted.

"We all felt infpired by the example he gave
"us, down even to myfelf," fays he, "the weakeft
"in the phalanx." Who now *uninfpired* affumes
an importance, that would have been ridiculous
in the ftrongeft. "I declare for me," he adds,
"I knew well enough." But how? He tells you,
"it could not be concealed from any body, the
"true ftate of things; but in my life," he adds,
"I never came with fo much fpirits into the
"houfe. It was a time for a man to act in."
And now he difcovers the true ftate of things.
"We had powerful enemies; but we had faithful
"and determined friends, and a glorious caufe.
"We had a great battle to fight, but we had the
"means of fighting; not as now, when our hands
"are tied behind us. We did fight that day and
"conquer." Such was the ftate of things, and
it was really a true time for a *man* to act in, who
knew he was fure of victory before he engaged.
And hence it appears, that all the formidable
defcription which he has juft given, of difhonourable and unmanly lords; of the houfhold troops re-
volting; of treacherous affociates; of earth below that trembled, and heaven above that menaced; of chaotic plots and counterplots; and of
the unfhaken fortitude of the minifter that con-
temned them all, had no exiftence. The minifter and his colleagues entered on this battle with
the unconquerable phalanx of a known majority;
which gave fuch *fpirits* to this orator, and proves,
that thofe, whom he would defcribe as *deferters*,
did adhere to his mafter. Or by what poffible
means could the majority have been obtained?
But now, alas! "*their arms are tied behind*
them."

them." Happy had it been, for this nation, had
they been bound on that day! happy it is they
ftill remain in bondage. We fhall now behold the
fupreme legiflative power; the dignity of the
king; and the authority of the laws reftored and
fupported in America; Rebellion fubdued; and
one general execration will be heard of all thofe,
who by delufive arguments, have excited them to
oppofe that fovereignty which they were born to
obey; and which it was at once their duty and
their intereft to acknowledge and preferve.

He continues. " I remember with a melan-
" choly pleafure," the fituation of Mr. Conway,
who made the motion for the repeal, " when the
" whole trading intereft of this empire, crammed
" into your lobbies, with a trembling and anxious
" expectation, waited almoft to a winter's return
" of light, their fate from your refolutions." I
fhall immediately attempt to affign the caufe of
this prefent *melancholy*, on remembering the paft
pleafure. But is the whole trading interefting of this
empire fufceptible of being crammed into the
lobbies of the houfe of Commons? Surely they
were either *miraculoufly* enlarged on that great day,
or are *hyperbolically* fo in this fpeech. But in
reality was there a merchant prefent, except the
American, in whom all confideration for the
dignity and rights of his country were fu-
perfeded by private intereft? It is reafonable enough to believe indeed, that their trembling anxiety and expectations were great. Since,
according to the words of this orator, they had
been crammed into the lobbies almoft all the *fpring*,
fummer, and *autumn*, waiting for the *winter's return of light*, to know their fate.

It

It was no wonder therefore, that being fo long
crammed together, like herrings in a barrel, when
" the figure of their deliverer was fhewn them,
" in the well-earned triumph of his important victo-
" ry in their favour, that from the whole of that
" grave multitude, there arofe an *invo.untary* burft
" of gratitude and tranfporr." What new kind of
gratitude muft this be, which rifes *againft the will*
of him who fhews it ? By what obligation was their
deliverer bound by fuch an *applaufive gratitude* as
they could not *abftain from giving him ?* But this accurate fpeaker contains an inexhauftible mine of
new and wonderful difcoveries, in the fcience of
human nature.

"They jumped upon the general like children on
" a long abfent father." I hope they did *that* alfo
involuntarily. Otherwife, the whole trading intereft
of this empire, jumping on a man's back, feems
to be a weight that few will confider as very expreffive of good-will. " They clung about him
" as captives about their redeemer." They certainly thought he had redeemed the money from
captivity that was owing them from America.
" All England, all America, joined in his ap-
" plaufe." I apprehend here is fome miftake,
at leaft, refpecting *all* England.

He then fays of Mr. Conway : " *Hope elevated,*
" *and joy brightened his creft.* That he ftood near
" him, and that his face was as if it had been the
" face of an *angel,*" concerning which fimilitude, as
I have never feen either an angel or Mr. Conway, I
have nothing to fay. "I do not know," fays he, "how
" others feel, but if I had ftood in that fituation,
" I never would have exchanged it for all that
" kings, in their profufion could beftow." What
will you conceive of that man, whofe virtue would
have

have thus exulted, had he been the leader in that debate, which ended in the flagitious immolation of the British sovereignty to American rebellion ?

But Mr. Conway has not persevered in that sentiment, as you are told by the orator. " I did " hope," says he, " that that day's danger would " have been a bond to hold us together for ever. " But alas! that, with other pleasing visions, is " long since vanished." Is it not hence that *melancholy* springs which attends the *remembrance* of that day's *pleasure?* His place, and all his visions of approaching greatness, even his hopes, are vanished. This is indeed a circumstance that may naturally depress a stout heart with *melancholy*.

He then says, of that ministry, " they differed " fundamentally from the scheme of both parties, " but they preserved the object of both." Is there not something incomprehensible in this, that a ministry should *fundamentally* differ from two schemes of others, and yet *preserve the objects* of *both?* Is not the obtaining of the *end,* the *fundamental object* of all schemes? How then do these schemes differ? " They preserved the " *authority* of Great Britain ; they preserved the " *equity* ; they made the declaratory act ; they re- " pealed the stamp act. They did both *fully,* be- " cause the declaratory act was *without qualification,* " and the repeal of the stamp act *total.*" The excellence of this *fundamental* difference in schemes, from that of all other ministers, I have already exposed to your view, respecting the *authority* of Great Britain. I will now shew you in what manner they preserved her *equity.*

Is it not inseparable from every idea of national *equity,* that the same *authority* should prevail through all dominions of the *same* sovereign ? That all his

sub-

fubjects should be as *equally* taxed, in support of the general welfare, as the nature of their circumstances can bear? And that you, the people of England, should not be more than proportionably oppressed in such taxations? Are not these the indisputable characteristics of *national equity?* And yet these preservers of British *equity,* suspended the executive power of parliament over the Americans; relieved them from taxes raised *for* their own support alone; and left you oppressed by enormous debts contracted in their defence, and exposed to the like oppression for the future. Such were their means of *preserving* the *equity* of Britain. Are these marks of those *sound principles,* that *enlargement of mind,* that *clear* and *sagacious sense,* that *unshaken fortitude,* which this orator did see in that noble lord and minister? Are the justification of such a cause, the falacy of such arguments, and the confidence of this speaker, such signs as can create belief, that he saw those exalted qualities in his master? Do these means express either a knowledge of *national equity,* or a desire of preserving it?

I have given him my opinion, and my reasons in support of it. Perhaps that may prove a sufficient answer, "if the principle of the declaratory act " was not good; he adds, the principle we are con- " tending for this day is monstrous." If, by this principle, he means the support of parliamentary authority then is it good; and so also is that principle, for which the ministry are contending; for both are the same. But should this question be asked him, since the principle, the right of the sovereign authority pronounced in the declaratory act is good, why did you renounce the ex-

ertion

ertion of it in favour of rebellion, what *would the adverfary fay to that?*

"If the principle of the repeal was not good,
"fays he, why are we not at war for a real fub-
"ftantial effective revenue?" are they not preparing by arms to obtain that end, if milder means
cannot prevail; and for another inexpreffibly more
important, the reftoration of the exercife of that
principle which, by the repeal of the ftamp-act,
was all but annihilated. By which act, the *principle* on which it was *perpetrated* appears to be the
moft ignominioufly degrading of national honour ;
and egregioufly exhibitive of broken confidence in
the executive power, that can be found on record.

"If both were bad, why has this miniftry in-
"curred all the incumbrances of both and of all
"fchemes? why have they enacted, repealed, en-
"forced, yielded, and now attempt to enforce
"again?" that both were bad arofe from their
being managed by this orator and his mafter. But
that this charge on the prefent miniftry, of enacting and repealing, has no ground, I have repeatedly proved.

"I think, fays he, I may as well now, as at
"any other time, fpeak to a certain matter of
"fact, not wholly unrelated to the queftion under
"your confideration." To the full as well now as
at any time, it is "that the court leaders have given
"out to all their corps this cant againft him, and
"all thofe who would prevent the miniftry from
"the frantic war, is that all the difturbances in
"America have been created by the repeal of the
"ftamp-act. I fupprefs, fays he, for a moment,
"my indignation at the falfehood, bafenefs, and
"abfurdity of this moft audacious affertion." I
will venture to affirm that no minifter ever declared
himfelf

himfelf of that opinion. They not only know and declare that the fact was otherwife ; but that the firft rebellion of the Americans proceeded from the fpeeches of *that* miniftry, when in oppofition; that their pufillanimous flight, before thofe rebels ftrengthened their réfolution of exciting difturbances in America; and that repealing of the ftamp-act confirmed them in their purfuits. Such are the known fentiments and declaration not only of courtiers, but of all men who can reflect and be honeft in their fpeech But it feems this man of mighty words, ftung with *indignation*, but *fuppreffed*, at fo falfe, bafe, abfurd, and audacious an affertion, rifes in refutation of the repeal of the ftamp-act as being the caufe of thefe American difturbances. And thereby he robs his mafter of the means of exculpation, which are offered from an inability of forefeeing, that fuch difturbances would be the iffue of that repeal. And thus he cunningly fends you back to proofs that cannot but evince that thofe difturbances fprang from previous opinions delivered by them in parliament. Such is the amazing ingenuity of this orator, in confuting the reports of his opponents, and in confirming his mafter's innocence.

Let but this low cant, infufferable as it is to·his *fenfe* of *honour*, his *love* of *truth*, his *averfion* from *abfurdity*, and his *horror* at *audacioufnefs*, be written as it was delivered, even by thofe who have fpoken it without authority, and it becomes indifputable *truth*. " All the *prefent* difturbances in America have been created by the repeal of the ftamp-act." Is there a man of common fenfe now living that is not fully perfuaded, that had Mr. Grenville remained minifter to this day, that the legiflative authority of Britain had been fully eftablifhed in

America,

America, by perfevering in the fupport of the
ftamp-act? has not the repeal, therefore, by the
Rockingham miniftry been the *certain caufe* of the
prefent difturbances? their harangues in parliament had caufed thofe difturbances which fright-
ened themfelves into that repeal. And that act of timidity neceffarily produced the fubfequent, acts to
reftore the Britifh fovereignty which caufed the
prefent difturbances. For once,-therefore, I coincide
with this orator ; that there were difturbances in
America before the abrogation of the ftamp act ;
and yet I affert the *prefent* were caufed by the repeal of that act.

Such being the iffue of his indignation, *fuppreffed*
in the charges of *falfehood, bafenefs, abfurdity, and
audacious affertion,* he virulently proceeds. " This
" vermin of court reporters, when they are forced
" into day, upon one point, are fure to burrow
" in another :" what a happy prefervation is vi-
fible in all his metaphors." Do vermin *burrow* in
a *point,* and are they forced *upon* the *point* in which
they have *burrowed?* however, " they fhall have
" no refuge, he will make them bolt out of their
" holes." And thus the *points* are become *holes.*
" Confcious, fays he, that they muft be baffled,
" when they attribute a precedent difturbance to a
" fubfequent meafure, they take other ground al-
" moft as abfurd, but very common in modern
" practice, and very wicked; which is to attribute
" the ill effect of ill judged conduct, to the ar-
" guments which had been ufed to diffuade us
" from it. They fay that the oppofition made in
" parliament to the ftamp-act at the time of its
" paffing, encouraged the Americans to their re-
" fiftance. This, fays he, a Dr. Tucker has de-
" clared in print. But this affertion too, juft like

N   " the

" the reſt, is falſe." It is indeed as *exactly falſe* as the reſt. I leave the dean and the orator to ſettle which of them is to be believed. And I appeal to evidence, infinitely more unexceptionable than that of both of them, for the truth of that aſſertion which this ſpeaker pronounces to be falſe.

I have already ſhewn you, from governor Bernard's letters, what were the opinions which the Americans adopted and purſued on being informed of what paſſed in the commons, reſpecting repreſentation in parliament and internal taxation. Altho' that be ſufficient proof of the preceding fact, yet I will recur to a letter which hath been already quoted, dated ~~July~~ 28, 1768. He ſays, " it was eaſy to be foreſeen that the *diſtinctions* uſed in *parliament* in *favour* of the *Americans* would be adopted by them, and received as fundamental laws. It would ſignify nothing by *what number* theſe diſtinctions were *rejected*; the reſpectableneſs of the names of the promoters of them, and the apparent intereſt of the Americans in maintaining them, would outweigh all authority of numbers for the contrary opinion. It was alſo to be foreſeen, that the Americans would carry theſe diſtinctions much further than the promoters could poſſibly intend they ſhould be." Will this orator now perſiſt in the face of this teſtimony, that it is *a falſe aſſertion*, that the oppoſition in parliament to the ſtamp-act, at the time of its paſſing, encouraged the Americans to their reſiſtance? all his appeal to papers on the table and to witneſſes produced in the houſe, and their ſilence on this head, weigh not a grain in oppoſition to the preceding letter which fully and irrefragably evinces that truth, which the orator ſo peremptorily denies. It refutes alſo what he ſays, when " ſitting
a ſtranger

a ſtranger in the gallery, when the act was under
conſideration, that, as he remembers, not more than
two or three members ſpoke againſt the act."

" The agents and diſtributors of falſhoods,"
he aſſerts, " have, with their uſual induſtry, cir-
culated another lye of the ſame nature with the
former." Which *lye*, to borrow a *mode* of ſpeaking, natural and familiar to this orator, will be
proved to be of the *nature* of *truth*. Let us examine it. " It is, that the diſturbances aroſe from
" the account which had been received in Ame-
" rica of the change in the miniſtry. No longer
" awed, it ſeems, with the ſpirit of the former
" rulers, they thought themſelves a match, for
" what *our* calumniators chooſe to qualify by the
" name of ſo feeble a miniſtry as ſucceeded."
That theſe three accounts ſhould be propagated
by the preſent miniſtry, can never find admiſſion,
but in the head of ignorance itſelf. The firſt report, "that all the diſturbances in America, were
created by the repeal of the ſtamp act," is over-
turned by the ſecond, "that the *oppoſition* made in
parliament, at the time of *paſſing* that act, was the
cauſe of theſe diſturbances:" *this* again was
overthrown by the *report*, "that the *change* of miniſtry was the *cauſe* of theſe diſturbances." Can it
be credited, that miniſters have ſet up theſe different and contradictory *reports* as men do nine-
pins, which, on one of them being ſtruck, it
tumbles down the reſt. Theſe reports are ſuch as
I ave been iſſued by the unthinking populace; and
gathered like bits of old iron and farthings, by
one who ſcratches in the dirt, and collects into an
old hat, indiſcriminately, all that he can find, that
will turn to any account.

In

In this charge of falshood, place but the name of *hope*, instead of *disturbances*, and all is right. For certainly their *hopes* of success did arise, and their endeavours grow stronger, on that change of ministry.

In this passage the orator exalts himself.. into the rank of a minister. He says, " for what *our* calumniators choose to qualify by the name of a feeble *ministry*." Does the word *calumniator* come with strict propriety from Mr. Burke? I remember a town in the west of England, where the pig driver, being appointed by the mayor, did always consider himself as *one* of the corporation. On this conception of his being exalted to that dignity, whenever he cried the pigs in the pound, he invariably concluded with, God bless *Mr. Mayor* and the *rest* of *our* corporation.

" Feeble in one sense," he acknowledges, " these " men may certainly be called." And from what has been proved, are they not feeble in every sense? " For," he continues, " with all their ef- " forts, and they have made many, they have not " been able to resist the distempered vigour, and " infane alacrity, with which the parliament are " rushing to their ruin." I shall presume to give another reading to the latter part of this passage: and leave it to your decision on which side the truth is to be found. " They have *not* been able to *continue* the distempered vigour, and infane ala- crity, with which they were rushing to *your* ruin." " Thus," says he, " are blown away all the *in- sect race* of courtly falshoods ; thus perish the miserable *inventions* of the wretched *runners* for a wretched cause, which they have *fly-blown* into every weak and *rotten* part of the country, in vain hopes that when their *maggots* had taken *wing*, their

their importunate *buzzing* might found something like the *public voice!*" What an admirable difplay of fertile invention, and of marvellous revelation in the animal creation is here afforded! An *infect race* of *falfhoods* turn *runners*, thefe *runners fly-blow inventions* into a *rotten country*; which *inventions* become *winged maggots*; which *winged maggots buzz* like the *voice of a whole people*. Oh! what a difcovery is here of a *transformation*, utterly unknown to all the philofophical focieties of the univerfe. Thus, like a fky rocket, from an artificial fire that urges him below, he mounts into the air, bounces, crackles, fparkles in a diverfity of colours, and then, by his natural ponderofity, tumbles headlong into the vaft *profund*.

He continues: " I have troubled you fufficiently " with the ftate of America before the repeal." of which one part was *after before* the repeal; " that of the difturbances, which were caufed *by* the *repeal*." I will difpute no man's right of *inheritance*. " And now," fays he, " I turn to " Mr. Cornwall, who fo ftoutly challenges us to " tell, whether, after the repeal, the provinces " were quiet? This is coming home to the point. " Here I meet him directly; and anfwer him di- " rectly, *they were quiet*. And I in my turn, chal- " lenge him to prove when, and where, and by " whom, and in what numbers, and with what " violence, the other laws of trade, as gentlemen " affert, were violated in confequence of your con- " ceffion, or that even your other revenue laws " were attacked? But I quit the vantage ground " on which I ftand, and where I might leave the " burthen of the proof upon him. I walk down " upon the open plain, and undertake to fhew, " that they were not only quiet, but fhewed many

N 3 " unequivocal

" unequivocal marks of acknowledgement and
" gratitude. And to give him every advantage,
" I felect the obnoxious colony of Maffachufets
" Bay." Whar a generous condefcenfion is this
to Mr. Cornwall, from fo great an orator!

And now you fhall fee his proofs of this tranquility, after the repeal. The affembly, in their
addrefs to governor Bernard, tell him, " if it is not
" *now* in our power, in fo full a manner as will be
" expected, *to fhew our refpectful gratitude* to the
" mother country, or to make a *dutiful and affec-*
" *tionate return* to the indulgence of the king and
" parliament, it fhall be no fault of ours; for this
" we intend, and hope we fhall be *able* fully to
" effect."

Did there ever exift an orator who more effectually defeated the caufe he undertook to fupport?
What was the caufe that " put it *out* of their
power fully to fhew their *refpectful gratitude* to
their mother country; or to make a *dutiful and*
affectionate return to the king and parliament,
at that time?" Was it not the durfturbances of the
people, which ftill continuing, intimidate them
from thofe acts of duty? The very evidence he brings
unequivocally difproves the fact which he undertakes
to fupport. In confirmation of this truth, I refer you
to the letters of governor Bernard, of Feb. 28th,
1766, and Jan. 20th, 1768, already inferted in
this anfwer, p. 14 and 15. In which it is faid,
" the ftamp-act is become a matter of indifference.
The people have felt their ftrength, and will not
fubmit readily to any thing they do not like."
This was the ftate of things in the colonies before
the repeal. After it, the fame governor declares,
" when the *imperial* ftate has fo far given way, in
the repeal of the ftamp-act, as to let the *dependent*
ftates

states flatter themselves, that their pretensions are admissible, whatever terms of reconciliation time, accident, or design, *may* produce, if they are deficient in settling the true relation of *Great Britain* to her *colonies* ; and ascertaining the bounds of the *sovereignty* of one, and the *dependence* of the other, conciliation will be no more than suspension of hostilities." Hence it is clear, that their hostilities were *not* then suspended ; and that the repeal of the stamp-act, by its fugitive timidity, had been the cause of their continuance. For rebels are constantly flattered by such concessions to persevere in their treason.

What a stinging reprehension does governor Bernard give that ministry, who thus afforded to the Americans, by the repeal, that cause of flattering themselves, that their pretensions were admissible ? But it was not in that mistake alone they excited them to expect the whole of what they required. In his letter, Sept. 20th, 1768, when some hints were given by the *present* ministry, that his conduct should be more spirited, he says, "in this spirited conduct I
" persisted, till I found it did not agree with the
" system at home, which required lenient measures
" and soft speeches, to bring about conciliation
" without correction. I knew that this would *not*
" do with the people I had to deal with ; but I
" could not dispute about it." This change of conduct was occasioned by orders, from the Rockingham ministry, to be conciliatory and lenient. And if fame be to be relied on, these smooth speeches were to consist of intreaties, that the Americans would be content with the abolition of the stamp-act at that time ; and with assurances, that the legislative authority was then suspended with full design to prepare the way for absolutely re-

N 4

scinding

feinding it at another. And that the declaratory act had no farther meaning than to filence their opponents in parliament, who would otherwife have prounounced them to have facrificed the dignity of the kingdom, in order to preferve themfelves in place, power, and accumulation of riches. Who are now the mumpers, that with a fore leg implored the provinces to be quiet? Where was the remembrance of this ignominious act, when this orator calumniated the prefent miniftry with that *mumping* meannefs which they never committed? And now, having reftored the *fore leg* to its proper *body*, I leave him to cure it as he may.

He now proceeds to afcertain the quietnefs of the province of the Maffachufets, and adds, " on " the requifition for compenfation to thofe who " had fuffered from the violence of the populace, " in the fame addrefs they fay, the recommenda- " tion enjoined by Mr. fecretary Conway's letter, " and in confequence thereof made to us, we will " embrace the firft opportunity to confider and " act upon." With what egregious indignities did this miniftry difgrace the executive power of the Britifh legiflature! They not only fneaked from before the rebels, but condefcended to make a requifition, for a compenfation of the violences they had committed; and thereby renounced that right of legally obtaining it, which the laws have beftowed on every Britifh fubject. Were all things quiet at that time in that province? Notwithftanding this anfwer, fo evafive of the requifition, the orator pronounces, " they did confider, they " did act upon it, they obeyed the requifition; " it was fubftantially obeyed. The damages of " popular fury were *compenfated by legiflative gra- " vity.*"

"_vity._" Ah! what a compenſation was here? Did legiſlative gravity compenſate for univerſal inſurrections? No. Did it compenſate for the violence of ſeizing and burning the ſtamped papers? No. Did it compenſate for the outrage of forcing officers to reſign their commiſſions under the gallows? No. Did it compenſate for pulling down and rifling the houſes of magiſtrates? No. Did it compenſate for the expulſion from their country of all thoſe who dared to ſpeak or write a ſingle word in defence of the power of parliament? No. For what did it then make compenſation? For _nothing_. Surely ſo ridiculous an aſſertion was never ſeriouſly uttered by human lips before this time! Sir John Falſtaffe, jocularly indeed, makes a defence, which in its import, is not unlike it. When the prince ſays to the knight, "ſirrah, do I owe you a thouſand pounds?" he replies, "A thouſand pounds, Hal! thy _love_ is worth a _million_; thou oweſt me thy love." In this manner you muſt eſtimate the _legiſlative gravity_ of the Americans, or the _injured_ have gone _without_ compenſation.

To this unexampled ſtroke of proving what he had aſſerted, he adds, " I am bold to ſay, that ſo " ſudden a calm, recovered after ſo violent a " ſtorm, is without parallel in hiſtory." After his boldneſs in ſaying the former, what may we not expect from ſuch boldneſs? As to the _calm_, if there were any, it muſt have been _during_ the _ſtorm_. For it has been already proved, that the ſtorm did never ſubſide. An aſſertion of that kind would be nothing unuſual in that orator, who has repreſented things paſt and preſent, and even impoſſibilities, to have exiſted together.

" And

" And now," fays he, " I hope the gentleman
" has received a fair and full anfwer to his quef-
" tions." And I, in my turn, hope the fpeaker
has received a fair and full refutation of his affertions. Which of us hath fucceeded in his endeavour, I refign to your determination.

" I have done," fays he, " with the third pe-
" riod of your policy, that of the repeal, and the
" return of the ancient fyftem, and ancient tran-
" quility and concord." To the policy of the repeal, and the return of tranquility, I fhall fay no
more. " This period," adds he, " was not fo
" long as it was happy." Short as it was, it was
longer than it was happy. For it is evident, that
happinefs it had none. Or there is no evidence in
facts. In reality, the manifeftations of impotence,
were fo confpicuous in this miniftry; the neceffity
of more able heads fo urgent; and the derifion of
their conduct fo univerfal; that they rather walked
out of power, from a confcioufnefs of infufficiency
to difcharge their duty, than were diffmiffed from
adminiftration.

He now informs you, " the ftate," *not* in the
condition he has defcribed it, " was delivered into
" the hands of Lord Chatham, a great and cele-
" brated name; a name that keeps the name of
" this country refpectable in every other on the
" globe " It may be called,

———— clarum et venerabile nomen
Gentibus, et multum noftrae quod proderat urbi.

Which being interpreted, may fignify, a name famous and venerable in all other nations, and
which hath coft his country feventy millions of
money.

" The

" The venerable age of this great man, his
" merited rank, his superior eloquence, his splen-
" did qualities, his eminent services, the vast space
" he fills in the eye of mankind ; and more than
" all the rest, his fall from power, which, like
" death, canonizes and sanctifies a great character,
" will not suffer me to *censure* any part of his con-
" duct ; I am afraid to flatter him ; I am sure
" I am not *disposed* to *blame* him."

Till now I never heard, that any man could be
canonized by a *fail*, before he was dead ; nor
that *death* hath ever canonized a character. Is
death a pope?

Let us examine how faithfully he observes his
promises. He continues : " For a wise man, he
" seemed to me to be governed too much by ge
" neral maxims. One or two of these maxims,
" flowing from an *opinion* not the most *indulgent*
" to our *unhappy species*, and surely a little too
" general, led him into *measures* that were greatly
" *mischievous* to himself, and for that reason,
" among others, perhaps *fatal* to his *country* ;
" measures the effect of which I am afraid, are
" *for ever incurable*. He made an administration
" so checquered and speckled ; he put together a
" piece of joinery so crossly indented, and whim-
" sically dove-tailed ; a cabinet so variously ir'aid ;
" such a piece of diversified mosaic, such a tes-
" selated pavement without cement ; here a bit of
" black stone, and there a bit of white." And
thus this great man, with all the eminent qualities
which this orator hath, in the preceding instant,
ascribed to him, is *now* reduced to be the
most ridiculous compound that hath ever existed.
He is a *maker* of *checquer tables*, a *speckler*, a *clumsy
joiner*, a *cabinet maker*, a *worker* in *mosaic*, and a
paviour.

parlour. Qualities which muſt inevitably have made his name reſpectable, as a ſtateſman, through all the nations of the globe.

But they were not *black* and *white ſtones* only, that he put into this pavement, " patriots and " courtiers, kings friends and republicans, whigs " and tories, treacherous friends, and open ene- " mies were inſerted alſo, ſo that it was indeed a " very curious ſhow, but unſafe to touch, and " unſafe to ſtand on." Why it ſhould be unſafe to *touch* is paſt my comprehenſion, although I agree it might be too ſlippery to ſtand on.

Such is this orator's happy mode of exemplify- ing the ſplendid qualities and eminent ſervices of this great miniſter, who is canonized before his death; and of *his* own indiſpoſition to blame him. " The colleagues whom he had aſſembled at the " ſame board, ſtared at each other, and were ob- " liged to aſk, *Sir, your name? Sir, you have the* " *advantage of me.——Mr. ſuch a one.——I beg a* " *thouſand pardons.*" What a vein of inimitable humour runs through this deſcription! with what amazing propriety does it delineate the manners of ſuch men! what a world of veriſimilitude it bears!

" I venture to ſay," ſays he, indeed he is in all ſhapes an *adventurer*, " it did ſo happen, tha per- " ſons had a ſingle office divided between them, " who had never ſpoke to each other in their lives, " until they found themſelves, they knew not " how, jigging together, heads and points, in " the ſame truckle-bed."* Theſe perſons are ex- plained to be lord North and Mr. Cooke, who were joint

---

* Imitated from the 5th chapter of the Bathos, of the true genius for the profund.

joint paymasters. The *elegance* of this passage is only equalled by the *pleasantry* of the preceding. It seems these gentlemen were two *pins* with *heads* and *points,* and these *pins pigged* together in the same office, and that office was a *truckle bed.* If then, in this high office, *they* pigged in a truckle bed, must not lord Rockingham's *clerk,* to preserve a proper subordination in ministerial *pigging,* have *pigged under* a truckle bed?

He now proceeds to give such a description of lord Chatham's ministry, that would stamp on him the most indelible mark of want of common sense that ever disgraced a man, and at the conclusion of it he tells you, " the most artful and most powerful " of the set easily prevailed so as to seize upon the " vacant, unoccupied, and derelect minds of his " friends, and instantly they turned the vessel " wholly out of the course of his policy, as if it " were to insult as well as to betray him, even " long before the close of the first session of his " administration, when every thing was publickly " transacted, and with great parade in his name, " they made an act, declaring it highly just and " expedient to raise a revenue in America."

By introducing the mention of this act to raise a revenue in America, the true motive of reducing lord Chatham to that state of mental weakness, in thus suffering the *tricks, treachery,* and *impositions* of the other ministers is disclosed. This act during his administration evinces this truth; that he then disapproved of the Rockingham repeal of the stamp-act, and of hanging up the sovereignty of England without life and motion. To obviate that oblique reprehension of lord Chatham, the orator with a spirit of ingenuousness and veracity be-

coming

coming his cauſe, hath thus traduced the character of that nobleman.

He then ſubjoins " even before this ſplendid orb was entirely ſet, and while the weſtern horizon was in a blaze with his deſcending glory, on the oppoſite quarter of the heavens aroſe another luminary, and for his hour became lord of the aſcendant." In this manner he has deſcribed the ſplendour and glory of that deſcending nobleman whom he had before in fact delineated as void of common underſtanding. In this he reſembles the profligacy of a ſon who having ſtripped his father of all his poſſeſſions, and allowing him but a ſcanty ſuſtenance, buries him at laſt with all the pomp of funeral pageantry.

This kingdom, it ſeems, was then illumined by *two ſuns* at the ſame time. Whilſt the old ſun was ſitting in blaze and glory, the new was riſing *on* the oppoſite quarter of the heavens, and thus he was getting *above* both heaven and earth, whereas all other ſuns had, and have ſince riſen *in* the heavens.

This ſecond luminary was Charles Townſhend, whoſe character he delineates as replete, not only with incongruities, but with moral impoſſibilities, as that of Mr. Grenville. " This portrait," he ſays, " was drawn becauſe the ſubject is inſtructive to " thoſe who wiſh to form themſelves on whatever " excellence has gone before them; there are many " young members in the houſe who never ſaw " that prodigy Charles Townſhend; nor of courſe " know what a ferment he was able to excite in " every thing, by the violent ebulition of his " mixed virtues and failings." In this manner this benignant orator aſſumes the office of *youth's parliamentary guide*, deſcribes Mr. Townſhend as

yeaſt

yeaft that fets all things in *fermentation*, and recommends him as an *excellence* to be *imitated.*

" But, adds he, he had no failings which were
" not owing to a noble caufe, to an ardent, ge-
" nerous, perhaps an immoderate paffion for fame,
" a paffion which is the *inftinct* of all great fouls."
Is the love of fame *the inftinct*, fhould it not be
inftinctive in all great fouls ? " He worfhipped that
" goddefs wherefoever fhe appeared, but he paid
" his particular devotions to her in her favorite
" habitations, in her chofen temple, the houfe of
" commons." This I believe is the firft inftance of
that houfe being confidered as the *favourite* habi-
tation and *chofen temple* of fame. It has been called the *temple* of *corruption*, a *chriftian chapel* converted to a *den* of *thieves*, and diftinguifhed by
other fuch appellations. But I believe the orator is
right in this new denomination. Becaufe it is fituated
exactly as the temple of fame was among the ancients. *Weftminfter Hall* is the *temple* of *virtue*
that leads to it.

He then adds, " that *befides* the characters of
" the individuals that compofe their body, it is
" impoffible not to obferve that this houfe has a
" collective character of its own." This is, in
plain Englifh, that the members have one character and the houfe another. " That character
" too, however imperfect, is not unamiable. Like
" all great public collections of men, they poffefs
" a marked *love* of *virtue*, and *abborrence* of *vice*."
And this being a character *befides*, or *more than* is
in them as *individuals*, they are, as fingle men, moft
abominable profligates ; and in the aggregate the
moft meritorious of human beings. And thus by
a fingular phoenomenon in moral nature, *each* of
them clubs his *quota* of what *neither* of them *pof-
jeffes.*

feffes. However, this is rare news for poor old England. We can have nothing now to dread from fo virtuous a body. Corruption is dead. *Liberty* and *property, roaft beef* and the *lord's prayer* are for ever fecured.

He now gives you a differtation on the vice of obftinacy, and exemplifies it in his own oration. To this he adds, " that Mr. Townfhend voted for the " ftamp act, voted for the repeal of it, and then " voted for the tax on tea, &c." And that he followed the example of thofe fpeakers in the houfe, " who had no opinions, no principles, no " order nor fyftem in their policy, no fequel or " connection in their ideas, as far as it could be " difcovered by their harangues. That he was a " candidate for contradictory honours, and his " great aim was to make thofe agree in admiration " of him, who never agreed in any thing elfe." What this gentleman can mean by contradictory honours I cannot conceive. How can any thing that *contradicts honour* be *honour* in *itfelf*, any more than that which *contradicts truth* can be *verity*. However, one of thefe honours is changing opinion with the times. Imitating the unintelligible in fpeaking is another. And thefe are, I fuppofe, among the particular excellences on which this *youth's gulde* would inftruct the young members to form themfelves.

There is one inftance of Mr. Townfhend's great excellence, in winning the hearts of the members, which is too confpicuous and inftructive to be omitted; as it is probably the only way that one in a hundred is able to win them. " *He bit the* " *houfe juft between wind and water.*" In this inftance of metaphoric tranfcendency, the *force of genius can no further go.* This image, with moft

moſt remarkable propriety, and equally inimitable
decency is taken from the ſong of

A tinker and a taylor,
A ſoldier and a ſailor ;
Had once a doubtful ſtrife, ſir,
To make a maid a wife, ſir,
Whoſe name was buxom Joan, &c.
The ſailor let fly at her,
And *hit 'twixt wind and water*,
Which *won* the fair maid's *heart*.

By this ſuperlative figure, five hundred and
fifty-ſeven *men* are converted into one *buxom Joan*.
Mr. Townſhend is made her gallant, and repreſented in the actual exerciſe of winning her heart
by a ſtroke *'twixt wind* and *water*. Without the
obſcene application, the words *'twixt wind* and
water to the fair maid, the *heart winning hit* is totally unintelligible. For if the houſe be ſuppoſed to
be a ſhip, and the members her crew, a ſhot 'twixt
wind and *water*, being the moſt dangerous that
can be given, can never *win* their *hearts*.

As this unexampled idea of winning the houſe,
deſerves to be eternally preſerved, I would willingly hope that the right honorable John Wilkes,
Eſq; lord mayor of London ; and member for the
county of Middleſex, will move that, at the public
expence, it be exhibited in bronze; a proper metal
for him to recommend, and peculiarly adapted
for the preſervation of ſo chaſte an imagery. May
not the fair maid be diſtinguiſhed by the ſpeakers robes and great wig; the mace under her
head; and the journals of the houſe compoſing
the couch on which the operation is performing-
ing, by Mr. Townſhend habited in the robes
of chancellor of the exchequer ? may it not ſerve
alſo as an archetype for a frontiſpiece to the

O

next

next edition of his lordſhip's moſt pious eſſay on
woman ? And now I beg leave to aſk whether this
winning bit of Mr. Townſhend might not have engaged the orator's fancy, when *he carried his argument irreſiſtibly into the body both of the parliament and
miniſtry.* He then tells you the repeal began to be
in as bad an odour in the houſe, as the ſtamp-act
had been in the ſeſſion before. It did indeed ſtink
moſt abominably in the noſtrils of all men of underſtanding. But as an *egregious ſtink* is conſidered
as a *ſource of the ſublime* by this ſpeaker, that could
have formed no objection to its merit.* "Mr.
" Townſhend moved for the act which placed the
" duties on tea, white lead, &c. and it was car-
" ried." And no mention is made of the duke
of Grafton's being at the head of the treaſury.
May it not have happened, therefore, from the
over ſcrupulous delicacy of this orator, that he
abſtained, on this occaſion, from mentioning his
grace; as *he* might conceive that miniſter had been
amply calumniated by *Junius ?*

There is one paſſage which it would be unjuſt
in me to omit, as it proves that this ſpeaker is
undeviatingly uniform in the manner of his figurative expreſſions. "While the houſe hung in
" this uncertainty, now the *bear bims* roſe from
" this ſide, now *they re-bellowed* from the other."
And thus the *ſounds* which roſe on one ſide were converted into *perſons* on the other, and *re-bellowed.*
" And that party to whom they fell, at length, from
" their *tremulous and dancing balance,* always re-
" ceived them in a tempeſt of applauſe." I confeſs I do not well conceive the meaning of this
tremulous and *dancing ballance* from which the *bear
bims fell.* Unleſs indeed pretending to be ballance
maſters,

---

* Sublime and beautiful, ſect. 21.

masters, and to dance the tremulous tight rope, they fell from thence into one of the parties, and were thus received in a *tempest* of applause.

The orator now returns to " lord Hillsborough " and the present ministry ; revives his old story ; " talks of the act, stating that it is expedient to " raise a revenue in America ; of a partial repeal " annihilating the greatest part of that revenue ; " of a secretary of state disclaiming, in the king's " name, all thoughts of such a substitution in fu- " ture ; and says that the principle of the disclaimer " goes to what has been left, as well as what " has been repealed." A long and tedious *repetition* of what he has already *repeatedly* spoken, all which has been repeatedly refuted. For that reason you shall hear no more of it. And then adds he, " I shall vote for the question which leads to the " repeal of both," that is the act which imposed the duties, and that which took off all the others but that on tea. " He now resumes the impor- " tance of a dictator, if you do not fall in with " this motion, then secure something to fight for, " consistent in theory and valuable in practice." Is not the legislative authority of this realm an object consistent in theory and valuable in pactice? is not this the object to be fought for, should fighting be necessary to secure it ? "if you must employ " your strength," says he, "employ it to uphold ". you in some honorable right, or some profitable " wrong." Is not that authority an honorable right for which this strength is employed ? and the *present* ministry do not chuse to desert or to sup- port the honorable right, which the parliament constitutionally possesses over the Americans, by following the example of that *profitable wrong*, which was done by repealing the stamp-act.

" Your

" Your minifters," fays he, " in their own and
" his majefty's name, have already adopted the
" American diftinction of internal and external
" duties. It is a diftinction, whatever merit it
" may have, that was originally moved by the
" Americans themfelves." The falfity of this
affertion hath been already evinced from governor
Bernard's letters. Thefe pofitively pronounce that
the colonifts embraced it from what had been fpoken
in parliament by the minifters whom this fpeaker
would vindicate, when they formed the oppofition
to Mr. Grenville : and this circumftance difclofes
the reafon for his transferring it to the Americans.
However, adds he, " I think they will acquiefce
" in it, if they are not pufhed with too much
" *logic*, and too little *fenfe* in all the confequences."
And thus by a diftinction as abfurd as that between the right of internal and of external taxation,
logic, is made to be one thing, and *fenfe* another.
May not this opinion afford fome reafon for his
manner of arguing ?

" That is," fays he, " if external taxation be
" underftood, as they and you underftand it when
" you pleafe, to be not a diftinction of geography
" but of policy, that it is a power for regulating
" trade and not for fupporting eftablifhments."
But when did it pleafe the Americans to underftand it in that light, until the arguments, urged
againft the ftamp-act, were tranfmitted to them ?
It has been already proved from governor Bernard's
letters, that, previous to that time, they underftood
no difference between external and internal duties.
And when did the miniftry underftand that it is a
power for regulating trade, and not for fupporting
eftablifhments ? For indeed who can underftand,
that taxation, which is the *effect* of power, can be

the

the *power* which creates itfelf? may they not as well underftand how a man may leap over his own fhadow.

"This diftinction," fays he, "which is nothing "with regard to right, is of moft weighty con- "fideration in practice." Why then, when the ftamp-act was repealed, did not that minifter pre- ferve the exertion of the fovereign authority, in that manner of external taxation, by an act of that kind? "recover your old ground, and your "old tranquility," fays he, "try it; I am per- "fuaded the Americans will compromife with "you." Shall the miniftry, to whom the execu- tive power is committed, compromife with rebels, refpecting that allegiance by which they are bound to obey the laws: or the parliament enter into compromife with fuch fubjects refpecting their in- dubitable right to fovereign legiflature? "confult "and follow your experience," he adds, "let "not the long ftory, with which I have exercifed "your patience, prove fruitlefs to your interefts." Experience has been followed. That experience which is derived from the daftardly flight before rebellion, and from the repealing of the ftamp-act. His long ftory can have no other reafonable effect than to refute all that he would confirm; to juftify all that he has reprehended; and to turn the fto- machs of all who heard or read him.

He now turns field preacher, and fays, "all this "is in the hand of providence." And then, not- withftanding he allows it to be in fuch unexcepti- onable hands, he would perfuade the commons to prefer *his* opinion even to a truft in *God.* For "now, even now," fays he, "I fhould confide "in the prevailing virtue and efficacious operation "of lenity, though working in darknefs and in "chaos. In the midft of all this unnatural and

"turbid

" turbid combination, I fhould hope it might pro-
" duce order and beauty in the. end." But as
providence produced, the order and beauty of
this world, out of darknefs and chaos, may it not
be as fafe to confide in *that* as in the *advice* of
Edmund Burke, Efq?

" Let us embrace," fays he, " fome fyftem or
" other before we end this feffion. Do you mean
" to tax America, and to draw a *productive* re-
" venue from thence?" what kind of revenue is
that which *produces nothing at. all?* " if you do,
" fpeak out: name, fix, afcertain this revenue ;
" fettle its quantity ; define its objects ; provide
" for its collection ; and then fight when you have
" fomething to fight for." By the permiffion of
this politician, the miniftry are advancing in a
more equitable and manly manner. They will
firft eftablifh the legiflative authority to tax ; reftore, to activity, that power which the minifter,
under whom he ferved, fo fatally benumbed ; and
then fix the revenue and what relates to it. But
it feems the fovereign rights of the realm are nothing to fight for.

He continues, " if you do murder – rob—if
" you kill, take poffeffion, and do not appear in
" the character of madmen as well as affaffins,
" violent, vindictive, bloody and tyranical with-
" out an object." Has not every precaution been
taken, and every lenient meafure carried into execution to prevent bloodfhed and deprivation of
property? in what æra, in what nation, by what
fovereign have fuch manifeftations of lenity, and
flownefs to wrath been given? and if at length the
fword alone muft. fubdue the rebellious and fanatic
revolt of thefe Americans, will it be *murder* to flay
the *rebel*; or *robbery* to take his *poffeffions?* can a
fovereign,

sovereign, his parliament, and ministers on such
conduct be deemed to be *violent, vindictive, bloody,*
and *tyrannical affassins?* no——the blood of those
who may be slain will be on the heads of that ministry who, apostates from their country's cause,
inflamed them to rebellion. And this speaker
may rest assured, that better councils will guide
them, than *he* has given, or can give. " Leave
" America to tax herself, leave the Americans as
" they anciently stood, and these distinctions,
" born of our unhappy contest, will die along
" with it. They and we, and their and our an-
" cestors have been happy under that system. Let
" the memory of all actions, in contradiction to
" that good old mode, on both sides be extin-
" guished for ever." Such is the insidious voice
of the hyena, which imitating the plaintive wail-
ings of a child, ensnares the traveller to listen
and be devoured. The true meaning of it is,
follow the steps of me and my minister, and restore us to some degree of credit by proving, that
you, the present ministers, are incapable of being
admonished by the misdeeds which we have committed.

If you, my fellow-subjects, still preserve your
reason, thus it must appear. If you are sus-
ceptible of sensation, you will feel this insult
on your understandings. If you value your
rights, happiness, and claim to equal freedom,
you will resent this insidiousness to deprive you
of them. If you are men, you will support
your king, his parliament, his ministers, and
your country's dignity. Abhor and renounce,
therefore, all those who have so long seduced you
to become the abettors of rebellion!

O 4   He

He then adds, "be content to bind America
"by laws of trade, you have always done it;
"let this be your reason for binding their trade."
But will you bind yourselves to be their slaves,
and to work for their ease and opulence? The very
tax he labours to repeal, is a tax on trade. The like
has been repeatedly imposed from their first charter,
in the reign of King William, to this hour, as he
has acknowledged, "do not burthen them by
"taxes, you were not used to do so from the be-
"ginning. These are the arguments of states and
"kingdoms." What state or kingdom did ever
argue in that way, and practise in consequence
thereof? Because, in the infant state of a colony,
when the constituents were few, embarrassed with
the difficulties of a new settlement in providing
food, raiment, and shelter from the weather, they
were left untaxed. Because they were so permitted to remain, during the encouragement which
was given, by this their mother country, in their
rapid progress to happiness and wealth Are they
after millions have been spent, thousands and ten
thousands of your fellow subjects slaughtered, to
procure and establish them in security, still to
be left untaxed? do *states* and *kingdoms* argue that
because their colonies paid *nothing* in tax, when
they had *nothing* to pay it with, that therefore
when they *overflow with a redundance of riches,*
they still ought to continue untaxed by that
very sovereign authority which cherished, encouraged, and sustained them during all their
difficulties and wars? That authority which
they never disallowed; to which they constantly applied for assistance; and from whence
they as constantly received it? What *kingdom,*
what

what *ſtate*, hath ever *argued* in that prepoſterous manner ? or what orator, but this, hath ever conceived them capable of offering arguments ſo repugnant to every idea of common ſenſe ? Yet ſuch is the opinion of this celebrated ſpeaker, who in every paragraph, even in his affected humilities, evinces that he preſumes himſelf ſufficient to the guidance of a kingdom. Hence ariſe his peremptory advice, his virulent reprehenſion, and his illiberal confidence in delivering his ſentiments.

" But," ſays he, " if intemperately, unwiſely, " fatally, you ſophiſticate and poiſon the very " ſource of government, by urging ſubtle de- " ductions, and conſequences odious to thoſe you " govern, from the unlimited and illimitable na- " ture of ſupreme ſovereignty, you will *teach* them " by theſe means to call that ſovereignty itſelf in " queſtion." This is indeed a ſingular and a pleaſant ſuppoſition. Deductions are made a *new* kind of *poiſon*; and then theſe *deductions* are drawn from the nature of *ſupreme ſovereignty*, to *poiſon* the *ſource* of government, which is drawing *poiſon* from a *thing* to *poiſon* itſelf. But that the Americans ſhould now *be to be taught* to call that ſovereignty in queſtion, after they have been ſo long inſtructed by this gentleman and his aſſociates, and are in actual rebellion againſt it, is really a ſingular ſuppoſition. And now he acknowledges this very ſovereignty to be *unlimited* and *illimitable.* The contrary of which he has repreſented in both reſpects, with regard to America.

" If that ſovereignty and their freedom." ſays he, " can not be reconciled, which will they take ? " They will caſt your ſovereignty in your face.". But on what does he found this *if?* It is on this

very

very sovereignty, and this exertion of it, the right
to be taxed by parliament alone, that we in Britain found our *freedom*. How comes it to pass,
that what conftitutes the liberty of Britons, can
be irreconcileable with that of America? And as
to their cafting it in our face, that they have done
already. " No body will be argued into flavery,"
fays he. But every fubject ought to be compelled to
his allegiance. " Let the gentlemen on the other
" fide call forth all their ability; let the beft of
" them get up and tell me, what one character of
" liberty the Americans have, and what one brand
" of flavery they are free from, if they are bound
" in their property and induftry by all the re-
" ftraints you can imagine, on commerce, and
" induftry; by all the reftraints you can imagine
" at the fame time are made pack-horfes of
" every tax you choofe to impofe, without
" the leaft fhare in granting them."
    In this page is there not a fmall miftake of *flavery*
for *petty larceny*, in the term *brand?* Neverthelefs,
I will allow him, " *if* the Americans be fo bound
by all imaginable reftraints on commerce, and
made pack-horfes to carry every tax that may be
impofed on them," that they will be flaves indeed.
But is a tax of *three-pence* a pound on tea, a reftraint on commerce that binds their induftry and
property; when, by that tax, they are eafed of
four times that fum, which they paid before? and
are they made pack horfes of *every* tax by carrying that *one?* As to their being without the
leaft fhare in granting them, in that inftance they
ftand exactly as five millions and half out of fix
millions of this kingdom indifputably ftand.
    He then adds: " When they bear the burthens
" of unlimited monopoly, will you bring them to
                                    " bear

" bear the burthens of unlimited revenue too?"
I have fully disproved the unlimited monopoly
already ; and if their revenues be no more oppressive than *that*, they will be the freest people under heaven. " The Englishman in America will
" feel this is slavery.——That it is *legal* slavery,
" will be no compensation either to his feelings
" or his understandings." What an *Englishman,
born in America*, may feel, I can not tell. But if
he do not feel slavery but from unlimited monopoly and unlimited revenue, he and his progeny
will be free for ever.

He then says, " Lord Carmarthen, who spoke
" some time ago, is full of the fire of ingenuous
" youth ; and when he has modelled the ideas of
" a lively imagination, by farther experience,
" he will be an ornament to his country in either
" house." I have some doubts whether the ideas
of this nobleman's imagination may want modelling.
My reason is, that this orator, in all his arguments, narrative, similes, metaphors, hyperboles,
and tropes has shewn, to demonstration, that he
is incapable of modelling ideas. But if his
lordship should be in that want, I need not intreat him *not* to place Mr. Burke for his *model.* For
if he should, is it not evident, that he can never
become an ornament to his country either in or
out of the houses ?

" This lord, however, says, that the Americans
" are our children, and how can they revolt against
" their parent? he says, if they are not free in
" their present state, England is not free ; Be-
" cause Manchester, and other considerable places,
" are not represented. So then, because some
" towns in England are not represented, America
" is to have no representatives at all ?" But I
shall

shall presume to prove, that the Americans are as much *represented* as the people of Great Britain, and are in possession of every right, respecting the election of members to serve in parliament, that Britons enjoy. It is universally allowed, that not more than a tenth part of this people have an elective right in the returning of members to parliament ; and it is equally certain, that these members, being returned, are instantly become the representatives of *all* the subjects, though elected by the *few* ; that they are as equally obliged to protect the welfare, and promote the interests of the former as the latter. An application to the representatives in parliament, is as much the right of the non-electors, and as uniformly attended to as that of the others. The Americans have always enjoyed, equally with yourselves, this common right of being represented. And in consequence thereof, they have applied to parliament, and received the aids of money, fleets, and armies. How then are they unrepresented more than all others who have no elective right? But it has been said, that all Britons may legally become electors; they are not excluded from that privilege as the Americans are. This assertion is founded on a like basis of untruth with the former. Every American possesses this privilege, equally with every Englishman. If he enjoy an hereditary freehold of forty shillings a year in England, or if he purchase it, he votes as either of you in the like situation. If either by the right of servitude, purchase, or presentation, he be free of the livery of London; or a freeman of any city or town corporate, where freedom gives a vote, he there enjoys the right of election equally
with

with you. Let him purchase a burgage tenure, or pay scot and lot, he votes from those rights.: and every mode of obtaining that privilege, in all places and respects, is equally open to him as to you. In consequence of these rights, we have seen Trecothick lord mayor of London, Sayre and Lee sheriffs, all born in America. In the last parliament Trecothick and Huske were members, Cruger in this, all Americans born; besides a multitude of others whom the sugar islands have furnished for that purpose. Thus it seems, with every right of Englishmen, they still complain that they are precluded. And whilst this orator, and others of a like stamp, are *exclaiming* against taxing these Americans, because they are not represented, they prove by those very *exclamations* that they are. For what does representation include more than parliamentary proceedings in this manner? And what seems not a little singular, those American-born members, whilst they deny the parliamentary right of taxing *themselves* in America, do without hesitation presume to tax *you* in Britain.

There is yet another plea which is urged in their favour: that they are taxed without their own consent; and may therefore be taxed to any excess the parliament shall please. By whose consent are you taxed in England? Is it by that of the electors? No. For they are never consulted on the imposition of any tax. Is the delegation of that authority to raise money, given by the few who choose, to those that are chosen, adequate to the whole community's being taxed by their own consent? Since five millions and half, of the six in Britain, are not concerned in that consent of choice, can the Americans justly complain of not

pofposseffing that choice, who are in the same predicament?

As an objection, to the right of parliamentary taxation, it is urged, that the Americans may be taxed when the Britons are not. Have not you been taxed *without* them, from their origin to this day; more particularly during the last war, to such an enormous degree, that you were mortgaged for seventy millions of money to defend their properties; whilst they were raising what sums *they pleafed only*, and for their own protection in America alone? But if that mode, of being taxed *without* you, be grievous; let all future taxes be extended through the colonies, and that complaint must ceafe. Appeal to this speaker's defcription of their happinefs and wealth, you will find they can afford it equally with you.

Such being the true ftate of the Americans, of what does this arbitrary oppreffion confift, againft which the virulence of licentious obloquy is fo egregioufly let loofe? Where is the illegality; where the injuftice in the exertion of the fovereign authority to lay duties on the Colonifts? But " they are " *our children* ; and when children afk for *bread*, " are we to give a ftone ?" When was this *afking* of *bread* returned by giving them a *ftone* ? Have they afked for reprefentatives? —— Have they not declared in the congrefs, they will have none? Is the *ftone* applicable in this inftance ? But when children are refractory; renounce their duty; and even oppofe their parent with force, are they not to be chaftifed and brought back to obedience?

"When this child of ours, fays he, wifhes to affi" milate to its parent and to refleft, with a true filial " refemblance, the beauteous countenance of Bri- " tifh

" tish liberty ; are we to turn to them the *shame-*
" *ful* parts of our constitution ? are we to give
" them our weakness for their strength ; our op-
" probrium for their glory, and the slough of
" slavery, which we are not able to work off, to
" serve them for their freedom ?" But when will
this child wish to become assimilated into one substance with its parent ? Are disobedience to the
laws ; a congress, subverting not only the constitution of the colonies, but of Great Britain also ; which acts with legislative power;
annuls the statutes of this kingdom, and
erects itself into the establishing of what they
please ; Are the seizing of the public money,
and taking arms against this parent, the tokens of
wishing to assimilate ? Is this the mode " of re-
flecting, with a true filial resemblance, the beauteous countenance of British liberty ?" To turn to
them our *backsides*, when they shall return to their
duty, will be as culpable as were this orator and
associates, when they turned those *shameful* parts
to them; and fled to repeal the stamp-act, &c.
But it seems this *beauteous* countenance of *true*
British liberty, is composed of *weakness, opprobrium,* and *slavery,* the *slough* of which we are
unable to work off? How *beautiful* is this countenance! how *true* this liberty ! And yet, all the
weakness, disgrace, and *slavery* of this constitution,
are to be imparted by an *exertion* of that *right,*
which we in England estimate as our *strength, dignity,* and *freedom;* that of being *taxed* by the *parliament alone.*

   " If this be the case," says he, " ask yourselves
" this question; will they be content in such a
" state of slavery ?" Such slavery as he himself
has

has denominated *true Britiſh liberty*. The very
ſtate in which you ſtand. Can *you* be *free* and *they*
be *ſlaves*, under the ſame legiſlative power, and
popular rights? let the Orator reconcile this contradiction if he can? let him, in juſtice to truth,
and to you, ſing his *palinodia*, recant his oration,
and prove that, by confeſſing his miſtakes, he intended no miſchief to this country? or, let the
criminality of his ſpeech reſt upon him. You will
be no more deluded by *ſounds* to oppoſe the *ideas* of
truth; and to acquieſce in the ſubjection, of this
kingdom and of your own rights, to the rebels of
America.

"If not, look to the conſequences," ſays he,
look to't, for thunder will do't. "Reflect how
" you are to govern a people who think they
" ought to be free, and think they are not." The
parliament and the miniſtry are now engaged in
looking to the true means of recovering a people
from the delirium of thinking they are *not free* in
the midſt of *freedom*.

" And ſuch is the ſtate of America," he adds,
" that after wading up to your eyes in blood, you
" could only end where you began, that is, to
" tax, where no revenue is to be found." Is there
no revenue to be found in countries overflowing
with commerce, in the midſt of eaſe and plenty,
as he has deſcribed them? where then are they to
be ſought for? but as by all the preceding parts
of this ſpeech you are convinced of the futility of
his judgment on things *paſt*; would it not be an
egregious abſurdity to liſten to his *prediction* of
things to come? "Lo,---my voice fails me," ſays
he, "my inclination, indeed, carries me no far-
" ther. All is confuſion beyond it." And *before*

it

it too. Hartſhorn! hartſhorn! for the Orator! he faints
---he revives---heaven be praiſed---he ſpeaks again.

"Well, I have recovered a little, and before I
"ſit down, I muſt ſay ſomething to another point,
"with which gentlemen urge us." Out with it
then. "What is to become of the declaratory
"act, aſſerting the *entireneſs* of the Britiſh legiſ-
"lative authority, if we abandon the practice of
"taxation?" This is a queſtion which, I think,
a wiſe man would never have propoſed, unleſs it
be wiſdom to ſet a trap to catch himſelf?

"For my part," ſays he, "I look upon the
"rights ſtated in that act, exactly in the manner
"in which I viewed them on its very firſt propo-
"ſition, and which I have often taken the liberty,
"with *great humility*, to lay before you." His
humility is great, indeed. "I look upon the im-
"perial rights of Great Britain, and the privi-
"leges which the colonies ought to enjoy under
"theſe rights, to be juſt the moſt reconcileable
"things in the world. The parliament of Great
"Britain ſits at the head of her extenſive empire
"in *two* capacities; one as the local legiſlature
"of this iſland, providing for all things at home,
"and by no other inſtrument than the executive
"power. The other, and I think, her nobler ca-
"pacity, is, what I call her imperial character;
"in which, as from the throne of heaven, ſhe ſu-
"perintends all the inferior legiſlatures and guides,
"and controuls them all without annihilating any."
Thus the *entireneſs* of the Britiſh legiſlative authority, conſiſts of *two diſtinct parts, and are juſt the
moſt reconcileable things in the world*. This, however,
is the capacity in which ſhe *ſits*, as well *reſpecting* England as the *colonies*. She ſuperintends,
guides, and controuls all the ſeveral inferior legiſ-
P   latures,

latures, which have been granted to the corporations of this realm, by patents from the crown; in
which predicament exactly and alone the colonies
do really stand. And therefore, as this speaker
declares, " all these provincial legiflatures ought
" to be fubordinate to the parliament, elfe they
" can neither preferve mutual peace, nor hope
" for mutual juftice ; nor effectually afford mutual
" affiftance. It is neceffary to coerce the negli-
" gent, to reftrain the violent, and to aid the
" weak and deficient by the over-ruling plenitude
" of her power." The executive power which
had been annihilated by abrogating the ftamp act,
and the legiflative which had been virtually abo-
lifhed by the declaratoy, were both of them called
into action by the ftatute which laid the duty on
tea. It is, therefore, indifputably right, according to
this opponent, that this legiflative authority fhould
be eftablifhed; becaufe it is effential to the conftitution. It is neceffary that it fhould be fupported
by every means of government; becaufe the
Americans deny that right, and are in rebellion
againft it. The orator, therefore, hath abfolutely
refuted all that he has urged before. He hath confirmed the rectitude of that meafure, which he has
fo vehemently decryed. He hath fhewn the neceffity of that law which he has laboured to repeal.
He hath juftified all that the miniftry have done,
and are doing. And he hath expofed his own im-
becility, or perfidioufnefs of oppofition, by ulti-
mately coinciding with their meafures.

" However, fays he, the Britifh parliament is
" never to intrude into the place of the others,
" whilft they are equal to the common ends of
" their inftitution." It never did. It does not
at prefent. The *common end* of their inftitution
is

is to provide for their provincial expences, as is
that of the corporate bodies of England. But the
universal end is that of contributing, in due pro-
portions, to the support of the British empire;
and this no corporation by patent can do. And,
then, in contradiction to all that he has been labouring to effect, he says, " in order to enable
" parliament to anfwer all thefe provident and
" beneficent fuperintendance, her power muft be
" boundlefs." Thus he proceeds even to defeat
what his own party have advanced. And to fhew
the inefficacy of requifition to the colonies he adds,
" the gentlemen, fays he, who think the powers of
" parliament limited, may pleafe themfelves to
" talk of requifitions. But fuppofe thefe requi-
" fitions are not obeyed ? what ? fhall there be no
" referved power in the empire to fupply a defi-
" ciency which may weaken, divide, and diffipate
" the whole ? we are engaged in a war ; the fecre-
" tary of ftate calls upon the colonies to contri-
" bute ; fome would do it ; I think moft would
" chearfully furnifh whatever is demanded. One
" or two, fuppofe, hang back, and eafing them-
" felves, let the ftrefs of the draft lie on the others,
" furely it is proper that fome authority might le-
" gally fay, *Tax yourfelves for the common fupply, or
" parliament will do it for you.*"
But he and the advocates for requifition fhould
know that no fervant of the king can legally apply
for national fupplies, to the colonies. It would be
an extent of the prerogative equally criminal with
raifing money by proclamation. It would be deftroying the moft effential liberty of Magna Charta,
and other innumerable laws; it would be laying
taxes without confent of parliament. Nor would
the mifchief end there. Such a requifition for fup-

plies

plies would at once impart a legiflative right to the Americans of raifing and refufing aids, if parliament fhould acquiefce in that application. For the very effence of a requifition fuppofes a right inherent in thofe to whom it is made, of granting or refufing what may be afked. Otherwife it is an arbitrary demand. If they refufe, fays the orator, then the parliament is to compel them. Thus you are firft to give them the liberty both of granting and refufing ; and then *compel* them to *grant* if they *dare* to exert their *right* to refufe. This is the liberty which he is contending to eftablifh in America. This would, indeed, be *flavery* embittered by the confideration of a *liberty* granted on purpofe to be fubverted.

He then adds, " this ought to be no ordinary " power, nor ever ufed in the firft inftance." The power of parliament is no ordinary power. And it *cannot* be ufed but in the *firft* inftance ; as is evidently manifeft. " This, fays he, is what I meant " when I have faid, at various times, that I con- " fider the power of taxing in parliament as an " inftrument of empire, and not as a means of " fupply." This is a diftinction fo refined, that it is either totally unintelligible; or fo ridiculous, that it cannot be fufficiently derided. " The *power* of *taxing* in parliament is *not* a *means* of *raifing a fupply*, but an *inftrument* of empire." And to what can empire apply that *inftrument* but to raife a *fupply* ? Thus according to him, that, which the *inftrument* can *only* do is *not* its bufinefs. And an axe for hewing wood is for the fame reafon not an inftrument of cutting, altho' it be applicable to no other purpofe.

And now he tells you, " fuch is his idea of " the conftitution of the Britifh empire, as diftin- guifhed from the conftitution of Britain." And thus

thus this realm hath *two* conftitutions. The fecond needlefs, and never till now conceived; or
one diftinguifhed from *itfelf*; which *diftinction* is to the
full as ingenious as the *exception* of *America* to *itfelf*.

However, he gives you his opinion, "that on
"thefe grounds fubordination and liberty may be
"fufficiently reconciled through the whole; whe-
"ther to fatisfy a refining fpeculatift, or a factious
"Demagogue, he knows not, but enough, fure-
"ly, for the eafe and happinnfs of man." That
is, by the prudent addition of turning that *liberty*,
which the Americans *now* enjoy in common with all
other Britons, of being taxed by the legiflative
authority, into a ftate of being *compelled* to pay
what they would then have a *right* to *refufe*. Such
are his ideas of liberty and legiflature. And now
to your judgment I appeal, "whether he has
"fhewn to Mr. Cornwal, that you are to lofe no-
"thing by complying with the motion, to repeal
"the tea act, except what you have loft already."
When by that compliance you muft flee from the
face of rebels who difpute the fovereign authority.
Hath "he fhewn that in time of peace you flou-
rifhed in commerce?" What prevents it at
prefent but the rebellion which hath been excited
by the harangues of faction in parliament? "you
"had fufficient aid from the colonies, while you
"purfued your antient policy." Whence then did
it arrive that you fpent fo many millions in their defence even in America? "were all things thrown
"into confufion by the ftamp act?" when that
confufion arofe from decrying in parliament the
right to tax America internally: and that it was
not only kept alive but encouraged, "when it was
"repealed, is irrefragable?" "what bad effects
"has the revival of the fyftem of taxation pro-
P 3   duced?

duced? what univerfal evil has the partial repeal effected? but fuch as evidently flow from that fountain which had been polluted by the oppofition in parliament; and which, according to the opinion of this very man, ought to have been undertaken to fupport that legiflative authority which Britain does poffefs, and which he and his affociates had virtually demolifhed? And now, let *thefe* confiderations, founded on facts, not one of which *he* can difprove, confirm you in that reafon which is fupported by experience. Can the long and tedious harangue which hath been fo amply proved in every fhape, fo nugatory and inept, be poffibly received as a confutation of Mr. Cornwal? every paragraph which it contains pronounces the contrary.

But " on this bufinefs of America, he confeffes " he is ferious even to fadnefs. He has had but one " opinion concerning it 'fince and before he fat in " parliament." In this very fpeech has he not proved himfelf to have been of *two*? he has afferted, " that the very image of liberty would be loft in America, if the colonies *were taxed by parliament* ;" and he has faid, "that *fuch taxation* is *abfolutely neceffary*." But mark his modefty, " lord North " will, as ufual, probably attribute the part taken " by *him* and his friends, in this bufinefs, to a " defire of getting his places. Let him enjoy " that happy and original idea. If *I* deprived " him of it, fays he, I fhould take away moft of " his wit and all his argument." Oh! what an exuberance of vanity is here difplayed! Edmund Burke, from the place of clerk to lord Rockingham, looks up to the pofts of Firft Lord of the Treafury, and Chancellor of the Exchequer! I will not recur to the fall of Phaeton, in order to admonifh
this

this *orator* of his rash ambition ; becaufe *Phaeton* was the *fon* of *Apollo*. Let him remember only, that pride and ambition were the downfal of Old Cole's dog. He *would* take the wall of a waggon, and was crufhed to death. It muft be confeffed, indeed, that this celebrated fpeaker does ftand moft egregioufly in need of *thofe two places* ; not only for the *wit* and *argument* which they include, but for a multiplicity of other reafons to the full as *cogent*.

I do verily believe that neither lord North, nor any man did ever conceive the flighteft notion, that Edmund Burke prefumed to be a candidate for the poft of prime minifter. It is an *original* idea, which no man hath at any time enjoyed, except that orator himfelf. But do you not tremble for the danger in which his lordfhip now ftands ? Was it not with a view of fucceeding to his places, that Edmund Burke, with fuch amazing propriety, threatened to impeach his lordfhip this feffion of parliament ? with what fufficiency he can fill thofe high offices, every paragraph of his fpeech, every action in which he conducted *his own* prime minifter, loudly declares. But fuch, it feems, is his opinion of his lorpfhip's iniquities, " he had rather bear " the brunt of all his wit, and blows much hea- " vier, than ftand anfwerable to God for embracing " a fyftem that tends to the deftruction of fome " of the very beft and faireft of his works." Does he mean the conftitution of this realm ? That I have fhewn to demonftration, he hath laboured to deftroy ; and which lord North is now engaged in reinftating. Does he mean the liberty of the Americans ? That alfo it is evident he would opprefs, by his requifition and his parliamentary right upon that again. In thefe circumftances he

ftands,

ſtands, and for theſe ſins he muſt anſwer to his God.

"But," ſays he, "I know the map of Eng-"land as well as the noble lord, or any other "perſon; and I know that the way I take, is not "the road to preferment." The road to prefer-ment is the *king's road*; and I ſuſpect that *he* is not indulged with a *key* to it; and let me add, for other reaſons than his *ſpeech making*. How-ever, "Mr. Dowdeſwell, his excellent and ho-"nourable friend, has trod that road, with great "toil, upwards of twenty years together. He is "not yet arrived to the noble lord's deſtination: "however, his tracts," ſays he, "are thoſe I ever "wiſhed to follow; becauſe I knew they ever "lead to honour." And to profit too, or elſe a man might wear out his old brogues without get-ting money to buy a new pair. Hence it is evi-dent, that this orator is willing to follow the tracts which lead to the honourable poſt of chancellor of the Exchequer. It is a modeſt ambition, may he be rewarded according to his merits.

At laſt he reverts to this declaration: "By "*limiting* the exerciſe of parliamentary power, it "fixes on the firmeſt foundation a real, conſiſtent, "well-grounded authority in parliament." And thus, with contradictions to himſelf, he concludes as he began, and has proceeded. He hath al-ready aſſerted, that this parliamentary *power* is "*illimitable*, and that it *muſt* be *boundleſs*." Thus *impoſſibilities* muſt be effected. That which is *illi-mitable* muſt be *limited*, "in order to fix a real, conſiſtent, and well-grounded authority in par-liament."

Such is the celebrated harangue of this popular ſpeaker. He hath liſtened to the enticements of

vanity;

vanity his Dalilah; he hath difclofed, by the publication of this fpeech, that his force confifts in
words alone. He hath flept in her lap. She hath
refcinded his ftrength. You may bind him with
a cob-web. And now let me invite you to reflect
on what has been offered to your confideration.
Are you not convinced, that an infufficiency of
fcience attends on all he offers; whether it be in
polity, legiflature, human-kind, hiftory, commerce, or finance? Is not his talent of reafoning
devoid of all true and genuine logic? Does it
fully amount to fophiftry; has it even the merit of
that *falacious* argument? inftead of imagination it is
animal vivacity active to unite incongruous and
impoffible images in the fame object; by which
afpiring to *foar*, he *precipitates* his *defcent* into
the fathomlefs *profund*. If you confider him on
the fide of declamation, are his endeavours attended with more fuccefs? void of fenfibility in
himfelf, his words are unimpaffioned and uncreative
of emotion in the bofoms of his hearers. He would
excite averfion from the miniftry; his language carries no fatire, nor calls up the leaft refentment. He
would awake compaffion for the Americans, but
every fyllable is inexpreffive of fympathetic tendernefs; it touches no heart. But in malignity without
wit, in derifion without humour, and in vanity without caufe or bounds, he is truly great. Review him
in the art of rhetoric! what is his exordium but a
flounce into falfe metaphor? his *confirmation* over-
fets the *object* he would *fuftain*. And in attempting
a refutation of Mr. Cornwal, he perfectly refutes
himfelf? His narrative, in which the fimple, una-
dorned, progreffive line of facts fhould be undeviatingly obferved, he ftuffs with falfe metaphor; and deviates into a delineation of characters,
which evinces, that he is totally uninftructed in the
heart

heart and head of man; and then his evanefcent per-
oration ends in a lanquid propofal of what is impoffible to be done; and which, were it practicable,
would be ruinous to the very purpofe that he
affects to obtain.

Through his whole fpeech, you have conftantly
before your mind the arrogance, the felf-fufficient
vanity of affuming the merit of all things to himfelf;
together with that infolent contempt for other mens
abilities, which difgrace even the orations of Ci-
cero; but not one ray appears of that genius which
illumines all his fpeeches, and fo amply compen-
fates for his difgufting felf-adulation. ——Hath he
not all the trafh of orator Henley, without the
pleafantry which fometimes attended his preach-
ments? In fact, is not his whole harangue a mere
play-houfe ftorm, that fulminates in founds, like
thunder rumbling from the muftard bowl, but
darts no bolt ; that flafhes in falfe metaphor, like
refin through a candle, but emits no fpark of hea-
venly fire ?

Believe me, he will print no more fpeeches.
It is not improbable, however, that he may ftill be
babbling like a young hound, on the fcent of
every animal, from the field-moufe that creeps
among the grafs, to the ftag that ranges in the
foreft ; and he will be regarded by the Commons,
as the babbler is by the pack, to whofe openings
experience has taught them to pay no attention.
But if he liften to the admonitions of unbiaffed
judgment, he will henceforth remain repentant in
one eternal filence in parliament.

Such being the true reprefentation of this
fpeaker's merit; the objects which he and his abettors prefent to your eyes; and the ends which
they would obtain, will you longer be deluded to
give

give countenance to fchemes fo difhonourable to your country, and fo ruinous to yourfelves ? Your fovereign and his miniftry have no defign but to alleviate your taxes and encreafe your happinefs. On that fubject, and for your fakes, permit me to indulge the defire of placing things in their true light.

That in all ftates there muft exift a fovereign and uncontroulable power *to do right*, no man hath hitherto difputed. It is congenial with the fenfa-tions of humanity. It is infeparable from every juft idea of national community ; and in this king-dom, the authority of *doing wrong* was originally refcinded, by the form of the conftitution. For as you the people, by your reprefentatives, conftitute a third eftate in the legiflature, it is a contradiction to common fenfe, to conceive that you can have delegated to *them* the right of enacting what fhall be injurious to *yourfelves*. The full power of doing what is moft beneficial to you, is that alone which your fovereign and his fervants either defire or would carry into execution. The power of inftituting laws, without that of caufing them to be obeyed, is an abfurdity too egregious to be fup-ported. If the legiflative authority be exercifed with juftice, in making laws; the executive muft be alike ftrenuous in their fupport, or to what purpofe are they made ? Otherwife it would be a mockery of government. The principal object of all fovereignty fhould confift in extending the fame laws with equal impartiality over all the fub-jects of the ftate. The next, that all thefe fub-jects fhould contribute, both in perfon and by pecuniary aids, proportionably to their natural and adventitious abilities ; becaufe a relaxation to *fome* is confequently an oppreffion of *others*, which is *flavery* in fome degree. Such then are the indisputable

difputable rights and duties of government; and
fuch as you have a right to expect from your
legiflature and your fovereign. By thefe I will examine the conduct of his majefty and his prefent
miniftry, towards you and the Americans.

When the ftamp act was repealed, it appeared
to men of found thinking, that unlefs the fovereign authority of this realm were actually carried into the colonies, the means of alleviating
your oppreffions, by obliging them to contribute
to the national fupplies, would be entirely loft. On
that account the act for impofing a tax on tea, &c.
in America, was made. It was furely the duty of
your reprefentatives to leffen your burthen, by
extending it on the fhoulders of all your fellow
fubjects. It was national equity, that pecuniary
aids fhould be fupplied by all thofe who were as
adequate to that fupply as yourfelves, and who were
not in a ftate of general taxation. This profpect
of bringing you relief, your fovereign faw with
pleafure. A fovereign, who by devoting his conquefts, both in the Eaft and Weft-Indies, to the
fervice of the ftate, hath proved by facts, his affection for his people. His minifters have carried thefe gracious intentions into execution. But the
Americans, inftigated by infidious men, were thank-
lefs for the innumerable affiftances which they had
received from you, in millions fpent, and thoufands flaughtered. After a war which hath fo en-
ormoufly encreafed their commerce with the ceded
Iflands, and eftablifhed their fecurity from their
former enemies, the Canadians; Poffeffed of
every right to the enjoyment of honours and advantage which you poffefs, they determined to
revolt from their allegiance; refufed obedience
to the fovereign authority; rejected the law which
was

was then made; set up a new government; pesevered in rebellion, and left *you* immersed in debts contracted for *their* salvation. Appeal to your own hearts, and if they are not divested of those honourable sensations which for ages have so signally distinguished the race of Britons, will they not applaud the legislature which imposed those duties; and bless and assist that sovereign and his ministers, who by acts of unexampled mercy and forbearance, are now reducing those rebels to their duty? It is *your* cause they now are vindicating! It is *your* ease they are now procuring! It is the cause of all posterity in which they are now engaged! These, and the dignity of the British empire, are the incentives to their conduct, and the establishment of them is the end they would obtain. Such being the true designs of your king, his parliament, and his ministers, can those who would oppose such measures, be the friends of Britons? By the incantation of the sound of liberty for the Americans, they would fascinate your intellects to assist them in their struggles for power, and then deceive you!

At the accession of his majesty to the throne of these realms, of every twenty minutes, hours, days, and years, you laboured, twelve of that toil were wasted, in acquiring that money, which is paid in consequence of taxes, on all the necessaries of life. In this wretched condition of oppressive servitude, these abettors of American rebellion labour to hold you still enthralled. Whilst your sovereign, the majority of your representatives, and the ministers, are exerting every nerve to free you from the chains with which you were bound in former reigns. Can *those* who would thus relentlessly bind you to eternal toil, be the friends of *your* liberty?

Be-

Believe not me! liften to the Americans themfelves, who from the congrefs at Philadelphia, in their addrefs to you, have faid : " *Know that in lefs* " *than half a century, the quit-rents referved to the* " *crown, from the numberlefs grants of this vaft* " *continent, will pour large ftreams of wealth into* " *the royal coffers ; and if to this be added the* " *power of taxing America at pleafure, the crown* " *will be rendered independent on you for fupplies,* " *and will poffefs more treafure than may be necef-* " *fary to purchafe the remains of liberty in your* " *ifland."*

Oh, that the propitious day were come, that could enable his majefty to alleviate your taxes ! with what joy would it be accomplifhed ! would that fovereign, who has devoted his con-quefts to the welfare of his people, withhold his revenues from leffening their oppreffions ? Yet fuch is the flagitious infult, of thefe rebels, on your underftandings, that under the ter-rifying idea of the remains of liberty being to be purchafed from you, they would delude you to unite with them ; and not only withdraw *themfelves* from contributing to the national fupplies, but pre-vent that royal revenue from being tranfmitted into England, for the alleviating of *your* burthens. That revenue which alone can annually diminifh your taxes ; gradually reftore to you every moment of your labour ; and apply every fhilling which you earn, to the purchafing of *things without taxation.* If you be men, you will manifeft your abhorrence of *their* ingratitude and treafon ; and oppofe with contempt and deteftation *all their abettors,* who would delude you, to fuftain their interefts, at the certainty of precluding all means of eftablifhing your felicity.

F I N I S.

www.ingramcontent.com/pod-product-compliance
Lightning Source LLC
Chambersburg PA
CBHW030318270326
41926CB00010B/1417